FOUL DEEDS AND SUSPICIOUS DEATHS IN LIVERPOOL

FOUL DEEDS AND SUSPICIOUS DEATHS Series

Wharncliffe's *Foul Deeds and Suspicious Deaths* series explores, in detail, crimes of passion, brutal murders and foul misdemeanours from early modern times to the present day. Victorian street crime, mysterious death and modern murders tell tales where passion, jealousy and social deprivation brought unexpected violence to those involved. From unexplained death and suicide to murder and manslaughter, the books provide a fascinating insight into the lives of both victims and perpetrators as well as society as a whole.

Other titles in the series include:

Foul Deeds and Suspicious Deaths in Birmingham, Nick Billingham
ISBN: 1-903425-96-4. £10.99

Foul Deeds and Suspicious Deaths in Bolton, Glynis Cooper
ISBN: 1-903425-63-8. £9.99

Foul Deeds and Suspicious Deaths in Colchester, Patrick Denney
ISBN: 1-903425-80-8. £10.99

Foul Deeds and Suspicious Deaths in Coventry, David McGrory
ISBN: 1-903425-57-3. £9.99

Foul Deeds and Suspicious Deaths Around Derby, Kevin Turton
ISBN: 1-903425-76-X. £9.99

Foul Deeds and Suspicious Deaths in and around Durham, Maureen Anderson
ISBN: 1-903425-46-8. £9.99

Foul Deeds and Suspicious Deaths in London's East End, Geoffrey Howse
ISBN: 1-903425-71-9. £10.99

Foul Deeds and Suspicious Deaths in Hampstead, Holborn & St Pancras,
Mark Aston
ISBN: 1-903425-94-8. £10.99

Foul Deeds and Suspicious Deaths in Hull, David Goodman
ISBN: 1-903425-43-3. £9.99

Foul Deeds and Suspicious Deaths Around Leicester, Kevin Turton
ISBN: 1-903425-75-1. £10.99

Foul Deeds and Suspicious Deaths in Manchester, Martin Baggoley
ISBN: 1-903425-65-4. £9.99

Foul Deeds and Suspicious Deaths in Newcastle, Maureen Anderson
ISBN: 1-903425-34-4. £9.99

Foul Deeds and Suspicious Deaths in Newport, Terry Underwood
ISBN: 1-903425-59-X. £9.99

Foul Deeds and Suspicious Deaths in and Around Scunthorpe, Stephen Wade
ISBN: 1-903425-88-3. £9.99

More Foul Deeds and Suspicious Deaths in Wakefield, Kate Taylor
ISBN: 1-903425-48-4. £9.99

Foul Deeds and Suspicious Deaths in York, Keith Henson
ISBN: 1-903425-33-6. £9.99

Foul Deeds and Suspicious Deaths on the Yorkshire Coast, Alan Whitworth
ISBN: 1-903425-01-8. £9.99

Please contact us via any of the methods below for more information or a catalogue.

WHARNCLIFFE BOOKS

47 Church Street – Barnsley – South Yorkshire – S70 2AS

Tel: 01226 734555 – 734222 Fax: 01226 734438

E-mail: enquiries@pen-and-sword.co.uk – Website: www.wharncliffebooks.co.uk

Foul Deeds & Suspicious Deaths In

LIVERPOOL

Stephen Wade

Series Editor
Brian Elliott

Wharncliffe Books

First published in Great Britain in 2006 by
Wharncliffe Local History
an imprint of
Pen & Sword Books Ltd
47 Church Street
Barnsley
South Yorkshire
S70 2AS

ISBN 1 84563 000 9

A CIP catalogue record for this book is available from the
British Library

Typeset in Plantin and Benguiat by
Phoenix Typesetting, Auldgirth, Dumfriesshire

Printed and bound in England by
Biddles Ltd, King's Lynn

Pen & Sword Books Ltd incorporates the Imprints of Pen
& Sword Aviation, Pen & Sword Maritime,
Pen & Sword Military, Wharncliffe Books, Pen and
Sword Select, Pen and Sword Military Classics and Leo
Cooper

For a complete list of Pen & Sword titles please contact
PEN & SWORD BOOKS LIMITED
47 Church Street
Barnsley
South Yorkshire
S70 2AS, England
E-mail: enquiries@pen-and-sword.co.uk
Website: www.pen-and-sword.co.uk

Contents

Acknowledgements

Thanks are due to Laura Carter who did the line drawings, to my friends and contacts in Liverpool who have helped with anecdotes, and to arguably the most dedicated true crime writer from Merseyside, Richard Whittington-Egan.

Acknowledgements for permission to use pictorial material are due to Liverpool Record Office and to Liverpool Central Library. For much of the sociological data, the survey done by the University of Liverpool in 1934 has been invaluable.

I have to thank Clifford Elmer Books for permission to use the Wallace case cover and the Maybrick illustration. Andy Tennick did several drawings also and talk about some of the cases with local writers was very valuable.

Finally, thanks are due to Liverpool Record Office for permission to reproduce images of Mr Aspinall, Silvester Court and Kirkdale Gaol, used in the Flanagan and Higgins murder case.

Introduction

For much of the period covered in this book, the city of Liverpool was like every other major city energized by the Victorian boom in industry and trade: a place with massive success and equally massive problems which came along with that. The Liverpool police force, formed in 1836 and lasting until 1974, was going to have its work cut out to keep on top of the urban problems it faced. Its initial manpower was 390 men; they would be busy, and would have to face all kinds of crime, some of it new, along with the new modes of life that came along with developing industries.

The new constabulary force in its central office had one indoor Superintendent or Commissioner, assisted by two clerks, and eight constables. In the day and night patrol there were over 300 men, including twenty-four inspectors. Forty-two 'fire police' also came along with this new force.

But of course, many of the troubles of the city were those of a past age, still surviving. One officer lost his life in 1853 at the hustings. Constable Sunderland was stabbed to death while trying to arrest a voter. We know very little else about him, and his story will be one that is lost in this chronicle. Other events have had to be left out, for reasons of space. The 1903 religious disturbances, for instance, in which a crowd had a mass brawl at Old Swan. Even more massive in scale is the whole business of juvenile delinquency. In 1916, the Liverpool Education Committee, appointed in a state of alarm over the number of young offenders appearing at the City Juvenile Court, reported that the punishment of whipping should be maintained. Of course, many fathers were away at war, but discipline had to be enforced, and justices were given the power to impose whipping on boys up to the age of fourteen.

But much more could be written on this topic; Liverpool was arguably the place of the reformatory. In the nineteenth century the city had the *Clarence reformatory* school ship for boys, off New Ferry. This was a battle ship that had been built in 1827. In 1884, it was to be burnt out in an arson attack by six of the boys. It was replaced by the *Royal William*, but that experienced a mutiny and a burning. Boys were dispersed across the land, many to the *Whitwick* reformatory in Leicestershire. In 1856 it was the largest in the country, and took many delinquent boys from Liverpool.

After the Juvenile Offenders Act of 1847, young offenders

could be tried at summary courts, and then, in 1854, reform-atories began to replace prisons as their destination. The rough, tough Liverpool lads who went to Whitwick caused such a serious riot in 1863 that eight constables were called out. One constable from Shepsted was seriously injured. That saga would be a book on its own, and any writing on Liverpool tends to have that effect: the subject expands, so great is the narrative potential of this complex yet wonderful city. It has the reputation of being a creative, bustling place, on the edge of Britain, looking across to America and Ireland. Its complexity is such that it has always had a volatile mix of races and religions in its demography. In the midst of all this, naturally, there had been crime.

This casebook could have started anywhere; in 1306 one Robert Clark of Liverpool killed William Walker, of the same place. Asked how he wishes to acquit himself of the said death and felony, he denied them and put himself on his country for good or ill. Robert had knifed the man in an alley, but in self-defence. He was sent to gaol to 'await the King's grace.' Wisely, the killer fled before he could be restrained and so became an outlaw. He may not have had malice aforethought in the deed, but he wasn't going to hang around and risk being forgotten in some rat-infested pit.

The nineteenth century seems the logical place to start, and a duel rather than an everyday attack is the first crime here. There were dozens of robberies of course; in 1788 a certain John Dowling and his mate Patrick Burne, were hanged on a temporary gallows. Their housebreaking and robbery had led them to that common end when, 'The emotions of the spectators were visibly many; men as well as women fainted . . .' The years around the turn of the century, when there was widespread fear of rebellion and sedition, were always hard and violent.

When the Industrial Revolution came along, and massive immigration took place, the social conditions were to contribute to a crime-wave and to the creation of many localities in which breaking the law was a way of life. The early Victorian years were extremely demanding and ruthlessly ruled by the capitalist im-perative. In 1841 the life expectancy in Liverpool was twenty-eight. One historian of the period described a typical profile of the Victorian city: 'Sickly infants living together in cramped, damp cellars made easy pickings . . . of the 350,000 deaths in England and Wales in 1842, nearly 80,000 occurred in children under one year old, and 140,000 in children under five.'

Yet the reputation of Liverpool people was and is that of warm, intensely passionate individuals with a firm belief in community and in the expression of life lived to the full. The poet and priest,

Gerard Manley Hopkins, living in the city in 1880, writes of the people in this way: 'Now these Lancashire people of low degree or not of high degree are those who most have seemed to me to welcome me and make much of me . . .'

The racial mix and the long history of immigration naturally play a part in the cases; and memoirs of life in the slums in years past often provide insights into this cause of opposition and division, though there have, of course, been plenty of examples of people of all races and beliefs living well together. Books such as Pat O'Mara's *The Autobiography of an Irish Liverpool Slummy* touch on this subject. This is full of tales about beatings, muggings, sailors being duped in the *Flag of all Nations* off London Road, and of course the ever present problems of drink, poverty and infringing the law. These matters deal with the larger questions in the social history of the city, and the same applies to one of the main characters in this book: Walton Gaol.

Walton is there as a presence behind many of the cases here. It has made the headlines for all kinds of reasons, notably the last hangings ever taking place in Britain: in 1964 on 13 August, a double execution took place there. Peter Allen and Gwynne Owen Evans had killed a laundryman in Workington. Their fate was an appointment with hangman Robert Stewart and his assistant Harry Robinson. The prison was built between 1850 and 1854 with a capacity to hold a thousand inmates. Its gallows were to be the ones at which Florence Maybrick was to die, but she was reprieved (in 1889).

The prison also became a focus for a scandal in 1892 when the Home Office became aware of the large number of women being committed to that gaol, and also an awareness by authority that there was very harsh treatment of these women going on there. There had been a problem of how one deals with violent, tough women, hardened by their harsh lives and inured to crime. It was not possible to whip them; they wrecked their cells. In 1892 when the prison commissioners took note of this, there were 8,591 women in Walton. Of these women, seventy-six per cent had already had a previous conviction. One woman, interviewed by the commission at the time, had been manacled with her hands behind her back for four days (and released only for food). The Home Secretary, Herbert Asquith, sent a letter directing that irons should only be used for restraint, not for punishment.

Before Walton, the name Kirkdale occurs in many stories; it closed in 1892. Its execution shed had been busy for many decades. In the earlier period of the nineteenth century, there had not only been concern about the horrors of hanging as a public spectacle, but also about the number of suicides following on from the macabre sight of a man dangling on the end of a rope. In forty-three days during 1849, the *Morning Advertiser* reported that after the hanging of Pulley, Sandles and Newton (in Liverpool), there had been a suicide and four murders in the city. Similar patterns were found in Leicester and Bath. As *The Times* noted in 1853: 'It has often been remarked that in this country a public execution is generally followed closely by instances of death by hanging, either suicidal or accidental in consequence of a powerful effect which the execution of a noted criminal produces on the morbid and immature mind.'

It is amazing that it took so long to appreciate the fact that hanging was not a deterrent and therefore influence government thinking. In the twentieth century, there were fifty-four executions in Liverpool. We have to rely on memoirs written by hang-men and other professionals to learn anything about this dark history, and there is more information available from James Berry in the Victorian period, regarding Liverpool. Only a few months after hanging a woman in Lincoln (Mary Lefley) who had to be dragged to the scaffold and was later proven innocent, Berry came to hang Peter Cassidy in Liverpool. He had beaten his wife to death after a night's drinking. Cassidy walked to the scaffold 'with a free, firm stride.'

The other main element in these cases, in addition to villains, police officers and hangmen, is the presence of the lawyer. The barristers and solicitors have their story too. The first assize at Liverpool was held on 7 August 1835, and the judges' lodgings at Newsham House were used from 1868. As Basil Neild writes in his memoirs:

> *Many notable figures in the Law have come from Liverpool and none more notable than F. E. Smith, the great 'F. E.' who became Lord Chancellor . . . Another great figure, Mr Justice Bigham, when he became a peer, took the title Lord Mersey, saying, "You see, I must leave the Atlantic for F.E."*

We could add to that the admirable Rose Heilbron QC, the first woman to have those initials after her name. Heilbron will figure in this book from time to time.

Perhaps unexpectedly, I have also included a story that might be categorised 'urban myth' – that of 'Spring-Heeled Jack'. He was certainly a criminal and a very unpleasant one. But in some ways, he has that characteristic feature of Liverpool, the tall tale. After all, no one is sure even of the origin and meaning of the

Liver Birds on the top of the Liver Building. Were they named after 'laver' – seaweed? Do they really fly at midnight when the moon is red? As a historian, all I can say is that sometimes folklore and historical narrative interplay so much that note has to be made of the improbable as well as the unspeakable.

What about the 'characters' and the celebrities? The history of crime and law always has these in abundance. In Liverpool, one might name William Prendergast, the DS from the city whose casebook was the resource stock for TV's *Z Cars*. Then there was Swasie Turner. What Alison Halford, former Assistant Chief Constable of Merseyside, said of Turner might be said of many Liverpool people: she called him 'a decidedly one-off, colourful, flamboyant, exuberant character..'. Turner began as a special constable in the 1950s, and then progressed to detective. His memoirs give a rare insight into the social history of policing in the city from the mid to late twentieth century.

My last story is from 1963. It was tempting not to venture into later years and look at unsolved cases such as the vicious rape and murder of Lorraine Jacob in 1970, at Mount Pleasant; and obviously certain major cases after that were potentially to be included, but discretion and good manners dictate that I omit these.

Finally, the reader will note that I have mixed notorious cases with obscure ones. Although there may be little new to say about the massive, internationally-studied subjects of Frederick Deeming, Florence Maybrick and Mr Wallace, their tales are so engrossing and problematic that they belong here, along with the domestic murders and swindles. Some of the cases are indeed examples of criminal history casting light on major scandals in years past. The prime example here is that of Thomas Peterson Goudie, whose story is the first ever 'True Crime' tale on film, figuring in Mitchell and Kenyon's *Lost World* film archive.

Militia Major Killed in a Duel

1806

. . . their animosity increased daily . . .

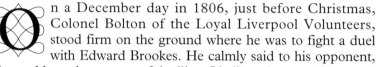

On a December day in 1806, just before Christmas, Colonel Bolton of the Loyal Liverpool Volunteers, stood firm on the ground where he was to fight a duel with Edward Brookes. He calmly said to his opponent, 'Agreeably to the custom of duelling, I believe that you, Sir, are to fire first.' Brookes, a major in the Lancashire Militia in former times, did indeed fire first, but missed his man. Bolton took aim, fired and in seconds, his opponent was down on the grass, the ball penetrating his skull, just above his right eye. The man's seconds and the medical attendant came quickly but the major was dead.

A good shot had killed a poor shot: a sad scene all too common in military history throughout the centuries. This rapid and merciless method of satisfying a debt of honour had given the Liverpool undertakers another customer in officer's garb.

Bolton wasted no time in removing himself from the scene. His friends had a carriage ready. As the *Annual Register* reported: 'Since then he has not been heard of.' This was wilful murder in the criminal law, but here is the problem at that time in history: it was a military matter, often related to regimental pride and honour. The law of the land was often at odds with army thinking.

Fighting a duel over a matter of honour had always been a principle element of British military life up to the Regency period, and such combats presented problems. This Liverpool case was no different. A war was being fought in Europe at the time against Napoleon of course; the military men were used to hard living, and their habits were carried over into civilian life. Army regulations stated that a man must defend his honour. Only three years before Bolton's killing of Brookes, a Captain Macnamara in the Royal Navy had killed a man in a duel and his defence was that 'he needed to sustain his character for courage.' He was acquitted. There had been a law passed in 1803, and known as Lord Ellenborough's Act, which made duelling a capital offence; if one

A TREATISE

ON DUELLING;

TOGETHER WITH THE

Annals of Chivalry,

THE

ORDEAL TRIAL, AND JUDICIAL COMBAT,

FROM THE EARLIEST TIMES.

By ABRAHAM BOSQUETT, Esq.

Qui ante non cavet, post dolebit.
Ay me ! what perils do environ
The man that meddles with cold iron ;
HUDIBRAS.

LONDON

1818.

Frontispiece from *A Treatise on Duelling*, 1818. Author's collection

participant was killed, then the charge was murder. But a law on the Statute Book is one thing: actual convention and army practice is another.

Yes, a killing like this was wilful murder, but someone would have to agree to take on the case, and he would be pitted against a massive groundswell of feeling that such an event was in some way 'just' and that honour was a personal matter, seen by many as entirely separate from any concepts in the criminal law. The two men involved were not only officers and therefore gentlemen, but businessmen in Liverpool society and known throughout Lancashire. Most likely, Brookes would have been seen as the least admirable, subject to the petulant and irrational behaviour that had him in its grasp for a long time before this fatal dawn appointment with death.

If Brookes' relatives wanted to press charges against Bolton, they would have had to do what a Mr Garrow applied to do to conduct a criminal proceeding against a man who had written a letter trying to provoke a duel, saying:

Sir, I have been informed of your unwarrantable conduct in forcing my gate, which you found locked. I suppose you thought it a public road; but that point shall be decided in a court of law. Now, Sir, I have only to add that I consider it a personal insult to myself and expect the satisfaction of a man of honour . . .

This was in 1815. It was not uncommon; one person at the time counted 172 duels fought in England between 1760 and 1821, but the military historian Richard Holmes considers this an underestimate. But the habit persisted

LAW REPORT.

COURT OF KING's BENCH. WEDNESDAY, NOV. 6.

THE KING v. RALPH SHELDON, ESQ.

Mr. ERSKINE applied for leave to file a criminal information against this person, for sending a letter to Thomas Dickins, Esq; a Barrister of that Court, with an intent to provoke him to fight a duel. It appeared by the affidavit of the Prosecutor, that he was on a journey to pay a visit to an uncle in the country, and in passing through the inclosures belonging to the Defendant, he arrived at a gate which was fastened, and, considering it a public way, he forced the lock. Having some acquaintance with the Defendant, he had intended the next morning to have sent a letter apologizing for this conduct; but before he could accomplish the design, he received the following note from Mr. Sheldon :—

"Sir,—I was yesterday evening informed of your unwarrantable and insolent conduct in forcing my gate, which you found locked. I suppose you thought it a public road; but that point shall be decided in a Court of Law. Now, Sir, I have only to add, that I consider it a personal insult to myself, and expect the satisfaction of a man of honour.
(Signed)   "R. SHELDON."

On the ensuing day Mr. Dickins, without taking any serious notice of this intemperate behaviour, wrote the following answer to Mr. Sheldon :—

"Sir,—I got home late last night, and were it not for one or two rash expressions in your letter, I should have sooner explained. I always considered it a public right of way, and nothing could be farther from my thoughts than to give you any personal offence.   (Signed)   "T. DICKENS."

Notwithstanding this forbearance, Mr. Dickins again received the following note from the Defendant :—

"Sir,—There were no expressions in my letter, which your proceedings do not warrant: you could not have done a more ungentlemanly act; my conduct has the concurrence of all my friends. You may beat down my gates, but you cannot make a Gentleman put up with an insult. You must beg my pardon, or I am determined to take the only alternative of which a man of honour can avail himself.
(Signed)   R. SHELDON."

Lord ELLENBOROUGH—"You may take a rule to shew cause."

Law report from *The Times*, 1805, re a gentleman's grudge.
Author's collection

for much longer than the legal attempts to tackle the problem. The law was ambiguous on the matter because duelling could in no way be interpreted as manslaughter, but manslaughter had been used as a defence until 1822 when the laws on manslaughter were revised. For these reasons, Colonel Bolton, running away into anonymity from Liverpool after killing Brookes was playing it safe, just in case he ended up in court. The judgement there may well have been wilful murder. But the duels continued until the last one was fought in Englefield Green, near Egham in 1852, with a fatality.

What had Brookes and Bolton argued about? We know that they started the dispute late in 1805 and that it was 'a matter of business' as *The Gentleman's Magazine* reported. Bolton was the chairman of a business concern in which Brookes had invested his money, and Major Brookes was extremely critical of Bolton's behaviour in that position. The argument was so fierce that they agreed on fighting a duel but others stepped in to intervene, and they were bound over, under a heavy penalty, to keep the peace for a year. Major Brookes could not let things rest, and he simmered with aggression and hatred until the period elapsed, then presented the challenge again.

They met at five in the morning, 20 December, on the outskirts of Liverpool. The fatal encounter then took place. Clearly, Brookes was not much of a marksman and, as was the custom when a shot missed, he had to stand with amazing courage, and let Bolton take his time to aim at the forehead; at least it was a speedy death. The tale is one of sheer impassioned hatred; a reporter at the time said that their animosity 'increased daily' over the penalty period.

Why did this savage custom last for so long? Simply, because there was then no legal redress for 'debts of honour' and this happened when the members of the militia were accustomed to living according to rules openly at odds with statute law.

It took several decades more after these events in Liverpool for a change of general attitudes, notions of masculinity had to change, and that was far more difficult to achieve than legislation, as was the case with the abolition of slavery for instance; the letter of the law takes a long time to percolate through to deep mind-sets and entrenched definitions of such things as 'honour.'

CHAPTER 2

The Hope Street Gang and the Cholera Riots

1826–1832

It was a panic generated by a genuinely horrific discovery

T he names Burke and Hare have not only attained the status of infamy and notoriety in the history of crime: one of them gave the English language a terrible new word in the years after his death in 1829. A 'Burker' became a word signifying that lowest of all killers perhaps, a

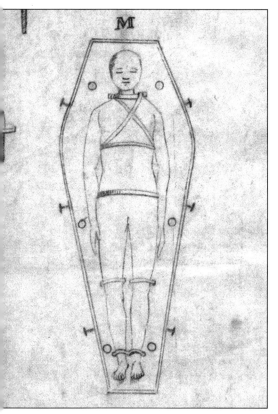

'Resurrection Man', someone who was willing to kill in order to earn some money from the doctors who needed cadavers for their schools of surgery and anatomy. The two villains had started their horrendous trade in 1827 when an old pensioner who owed them £4 was killed and taken to Dr Knox's anatomy school in Edinburgh. For his corpse, they received over £7 – much more than the sum he owed them.

Clearly, this was a quick and easy way to earn some cash, so Burke and Hare developed their business into a murderous enterprise targeting tramps and prostitutes. But it led Burke to the gallows and Hare to a runaway life as a poor fugitive in

An early Victorian device for defying bodysnatchers. Author's collection

London. Unfortunately for the poor and vulnerable of other cities in Britain, the trade in bodies had an appeal to other 'Burkers' and Liverpool had its own gang of these desperate individuals.

In 1826, some dockers at the St George's Dock began to complain about the intolerable smell coming from some containers labelled 'Bitter Salts' which were scheduled to be shipped to the port of Leith. Things came to a head and the stench was so bad that the boxes had to be opened. What met their eyes was totally repugnant and shocking: inside were eleven naked corpses, preserved in brine (following the long tradition of salting bodies as in ancient Egypt), and this led to further investigations at number eleven, Hope Street, where more than twenty other corpses were found, some preserved by hot wax injection. There had even been some bodies of dead infants preserved in brine. The consequences of this find were to lead to large-scale riots and social disorder, mostly based on the arrival of cholera in the town, and on the nefarious actions of a doctor, William Gill, who had been organising 'resurrection' business for the anatomy schools.

At the trial of the gang, and notably of James Donaldson who was the overall manager of the business, there was a furore when the subject of the children's bodies was discussed. As the *Liverpool Mercury* reported:

> *One of the witnesses stated, that in the cellar there was a tierce [a vessel holding two-thirds of a hogshead of liquid] containing a quantity of brine which they poured off, and found the bodies of some babies . . . an audible shudder ran through the court on the mention of this last circumstance and the foreman of the jury was taken suddenly ill . . .*

Donaldson was put in prison for a year and had to pay a fine of £50. The whole business was sickening, and more was to come when another man was arrested in relation to containers with corpses in them, and this person had parish cemetery keys on his person – keys to the door of a vault. In 1827 there was more grave-robbing going on at Walton Church. At the home of local surgeon William Gill five bodies were found; someone had seen some grave-robbing actually happening and this led to the investigation and the arrest of the doctor. At Gill's trial, the issue of the medical problem of having to have access to bodies for dissection was prominent. He even read a long statement at his trial, defending his actions in terms of a professional reason for why he had been driven to do. He avoided a custodial sentence and was fined £30.

Hope Street today. The author

After the actual dissection and Burking scandals, the issue at the centre of all this became related to the arrival of Asiatic cholera in the city. In 1831 Liverpool's population was in a state of public health crisis but not much was being done; a massive Irish immigration had contributed to this. One estimate calculates that over half a million Irish people arrived in Liverpool on the first half of the nineteenth century. Of course, some of these would carry on and board ships for America but, nevertheless, the population expanded rapidly and many poor workers lived in overcrowded homes and cellars. There were to be almost 5,000 cases of cholera in the city during the crisis years of the 1830s, and around thirty-one per cent were fatal.

In 1832, there were several signs that Asiatic cholera had come to Liverpool, but the Board of Health and its advisers tried to deny this. One of the most shameful episodes here is that the Board was given a large sum of money when it cleared vessels to leave port with a clean bill of health, and had been doing so for some time before the truth was out in the streets that cholera had come and that the belief grew that medical men were using the bodies of people dying from the disease for anatomical study. One sensation that highlighted the attempt to ignore the problem was the out-break of cholera on board the *Brutus*, a ship that set sail from Liverpool in May 1832. As the *Annual Register* reported at the time:

> *On the 27th, the ninth day out of Liverpool, a healthy man, about thirty years of age, was seized with malignant cholera. The usual remedies were used and he recovered. The next case was a sixty year old woman, who died in ten hours of the attack . . . The ravages of the pestilence then increased . . . The greatest number of deaths was twenty-four in one day . . .*

There was a string of violent riots in the city, starting in May 1832, when there was a frightening attack on the Toxteth Park Cholera Hospital. The *Chronicle* reported that a mob surrounded a patient and accompanying staff as he was bound for the hospital and began raising hell. When the patient was taken inside, the mob still raged outside, shouting 'Bring out the Burkers!' Things carried on in this way for a month. In Lime Street, a woman was attacked, accused of being a Burker and, luckily, found a place to

Memorial plaque to Dr W H Duncan, Rodney Street. The author

hide; then there were several more disturbances in the city centre, and one in the dock area, at Barter Street. In all there were eight riots across most parts of Liverpool.

In this same year, the Anatomy Act had been passed; this was the first attempt to try to make cadavers available to medical research, and cut out the need for illicit trade. The idea was to make the bodies of paupers available for use: those people who would be unclaimed by their family. Even that was slow to find its way through parliament, as Henry Warburton had produced the bill in 1829, but it took three years to be made into law. In those three years the riots in the regions had continued. The disgusting

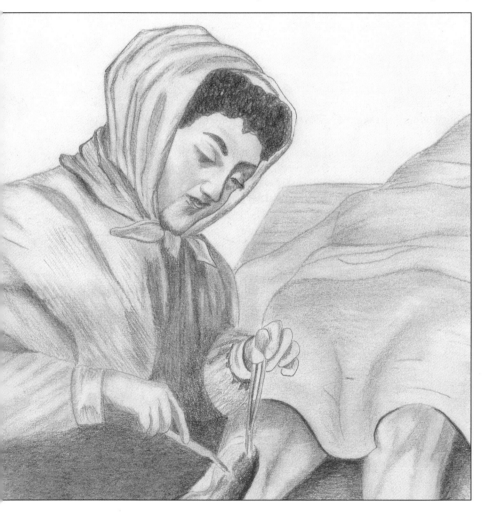

A young female medical student performing a dissection. Andy Tennick

sensation of 'The Italian Boy' in London, a case which ended in the hanging of two Burkers, with a crowd of 100,000 people watching them die, made body-snatching very big news indeed, reaching into the provinces. The two villains had killed sixteen people for profit.

The cholera riots in Liverpool finally stopped in June. The Mayor had received a letter from 'an Irishman' threatening that there would be awful consequences if he did not act. A meeting was called in which the Board of Health talked to the city's Catholic priests, and then shortly after an announcement was made in all the churches. The aim was to allay fears about the alleged Burking in the cellars and port. The important part of the statement was that bodies after death would be seen by family:

> . . . *orders have been issued that the relations of those who die in the hospital shall be allowed to see the bodies of the deceased before the coffins are closed, and that they may within a limited time take them away to the grave. Permission is also granted to relatives of the sick to see them in hospital daily, under certain regulations necessary for preventing infections.*

Some historians have pinpointed the year 1831 as the time when Britain was coming very close to revolution; the agitation for what was to be the great Reform Act the next year was part of this, and so were the various kinds of labour unrest. But the cholera riots in Liverpool and other cities formed a major part of that feeling at the time that life was experienced 'on the edge' of disaster and ruin. The papers at the time tried to blame the trouble on 'the Irish' and on the destitute poor, but these were grossly unfair and wrong-headed. It was a panic instigated by a genuinely horrific discovery, and the fact that respected medical men had been involved, and that they had been fined in court, only added to the sense of outrage in the streets.

But the study of medicine and the necessity for doctors to be trained in Anatomy, meant that the dissections had to go on, as they always had; the old prints and illustrations show the importance of this advancing knowledge in the fight against disease.

CHAPTER 3

A Poacher Shooting

1846

The problem for Lynn was that the stock of his gun was cracked

Gamekeeper John Wainwright was enjoying a pint with his friend at the *Eagle and Child* tavern on 15 April 1846. This was near the Earl of Derby's estate at Knowsley, where Wainwright was assistant gamekeeper. This was about a mile from the village of Prescot, and it should have been a good place to relax, but at half past nine that night, shots were heard outside the pub and Wainwright sensibly went outside, via the back door, to investigate this with some caution. But the person out in the dark was ready, and when the gamekeeper reached the gate, a volley of shots was fired, some hitting him, wounding him in the leg and hand. When the landlord of the pub ran outside to see what was happening, the gunman was seen to run off into some of the woods belonging to Sir Thomas Birch. As Wainwright collapsed in pain, the landlord ran after the attacker, but he was soon away into the night.

But the shots were fired by a man who was soon traced, as a footprint was found in soft earth that night, where the gunman had run away, and these matched the show of the major suspect, Charles Lynn. He was soon in court, and witnesses who had been drinking in another pub close to where the attack took place, the *Rose and Crown*, said that they saw him take out a gun which was in two parts, and then assemble it. The problem for Lynn was that the stock of this gun was cracked, and that was noticed; when a gun with that feature was found in the Birch plantation, the match was obvious and the link to the villain was made sure. In the pub, he had been with a friend, and as they loaded the gun, his friend said, 'Put some of the others in, they'll tell a tale.' That meant that he loaded two kinds of shot, and he was heard to say that he would go out for game 'in spite of anybody.'

The man must have been amazingly reckless, because people reported that when he left the *Rose and Crown* he was heard to say, 'Let either Birch or Wainwright molest us on the road and we'll do their job for them.' Again, with crazy bravado, Lynn had been seen by a passer-by near the plantation and had been asked what he was doing. He replied, 'I am looking for a hare' and that he would have a hare 'and Birch afterwards.' No less than a pile of twenty-five shot was found in the doorway where Lynn had been standing that night.

There had been a series of game laws passed between 1671 and 1830, aiming to confine the shooting of game (mostly hares, partridge and pheasants) to those estates with a value of over £100 a year. Often poaching was ignored, or incurred small penalties, but it was for Lynn a far more serious affair. He had surely been attempting to kill his man. In the years between 1814 and 1834, for crimes involving 'shooting at, stabbing, wounding . . . with intent to murder' 359 people had been sentenced, and of these, 315 were executed. Lynn had staged his attack at a time only ten years or so after the revisions of the massive number of capital crimes on the statute books, brought about by Sir Robert Peel.

After all, it is clear from the facts that Lynn had been waiting for Wainwright, and that he had a grudge against him. He must have been in position, knowing where the victim was likely to emerge from the pub, so he knew the man's habits and then fired shots to rouse him. This highlights the uneasy relationship between gamekeeper and poacher at the time. If the shots had hit their target only a few inches higher, then the gamekeeper would probably have died from wounds. It is of no account that the background to this grudge was related to the common view of poaching as something other than a crime. The almost universal opinion among the poorer country people was that game were 'in a wild state, not the property of any one individual.' But the steps leading from that mindset to this one of an intention to maim or kill, was exceptional. The punishment was certain to be severe.

It didn't take long to find the man guilty. He was sentenced to fourteen years transportation. Technically, the offence was grievous bodily harm, an offence that was only truly defined within the Offences Against the Persons Act of 1861; basically, Lynn had been very fortunate in that the wounds had not been mortal on Wainwright. There was a fine line between attempted murder and grievous bodily harm. Only two years before, on the estate of Lord Derby, a poacher called Roberts had shot and killed a gamekeeper. Roberts and four others who were with him, and who did not fire, were condemned to death. An anonymous correspondent to *The Times* picked up on the anomalies in punishments for poaching, saying:

Again and again has the ruffian, whose act has really come so near murder that it would be scarcely possible to draw the distinction, and who at any rate has shown all the animus and brutality of the murderer, escaped with some few months' imprisonment, while the miserable half-starved purloiner of a bit of bread has had his seven years' transportation. It is on this very account that we take up this case at Liverpool.

The writer of this was puzzled at the trial of the four men for the murder of the gamekeeper and how it compared to other sentences. The letter was expressing the kind of weaknesses that the judge and jury of Lynn realised, and so his sentence was tough. What lay behind all this was the lingering doubt about the act of poaching itself, regardless of the fact that Lynn had gone to the *Eagle and Child* that night to settle a score. What would have irritated Lynn most of all was that he would have been subject to a fine of £2, as stated in the 1831 Act, for 'trespass in daytime in pursuit of conies' and in pursuit of game in daytime, £2, and if this was not paid, then the prison cell waited for him, for two months.

These petty squabbles and everyday encounters in situations where many people thought it was a universal right to take a hare anywhere and any time, in this case, led a man to shoot and maim a gamekeeper, even at a time when he was not on duty.

The severe penalties for breaching the game laws are illustrated by the reactionary acts introduced in the reign of George I, when the death penalty was imposed for 'Robbing Warrens' and for 'stealing or taking any fish from any river or pond.' Sixty-eight people were hanged for sheep-stealing between 1814 and 1834.

A Brutal Robbery

1852

The actual robbery could not be proved . . .

When a gang of footpads – William Mitchell, William Jackson and Sarah Brown – set about Thomas Tatem in the street they had no idea that they would present a legal problem for the judge and jury. One of the panel of judges was the famous Justice Maule, and he found the case to be a brain-teaser which he clearly enjoyed.

The three hoodlums grabbed Tatem and threw him to the ground, and then went on to take money from him by force, or so it was alleged. Although in court they were shown to have 'feloniously made an assault' – in other words, it was a serious matter with a tough penalty. There was a problem, as there was no prosecutor, and therefore no evidence that they had stolen anything. What was resting on the decision was that if they had done 'a felonious assault, aggravated, and with an intent to rob', they were liable to transportation for life. There was going to be a problem in sentencing Sarah Brown, as she had a previous conviction, but the men's situation was going to take some wrangling.

The issue was whether or not the gang had an intention to rob Tatem, an old man who could not defend himself. If they assaulted him without an intention to rob, then they could escape transportation. Baron Campbell at the Crown Court, argued that their intention was indeed to rob. He wanted the three of them on the ships to Botany Bay. What had to happen was that the jury had to understand that they could return a verdict assuming the gang's guilt in intending to rob as well as assault the man. Baron Campbell had only one stumbling-block: there were alternative sentences for the crime, dating back to 1837. One possibility was that the culprits could be given only three years' hard labour. The wigs were put on and the meaning of Lord Campbell's Act discussed. The arguments led nowhere and they gave in, putting off a decision until the next assizes.

They met again, on 29 May 1852. This is when Maule made

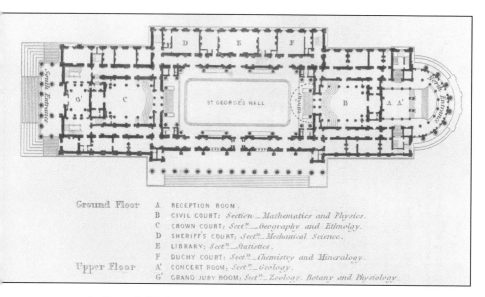

St George's Hall, from a plan dated 1857. Author's collection

an appearance, so there was to be a decision; Maule was recalled by another famous judge as 'A man of great wit, sound sense and curious humour such as I never heard in any other man. He possessed a particularly keen apprehension. To those who had any real ability he was the most pleasant of judges, but he had little love for mediocrities.' This time he took the view that the attack had been an 'aggravated robbery' – the victim had been 'roughed up' in the process. This was indeed an assumption, as there was no clear picture of the events.

Baron Alderson spoke at great length, complicating the affair, and when he ended, Maule simply said: 'The words of section nine of Campbell are, "if upon the trial of any person upon any indictment for robbery . . ."' He had a smile of satisfaction as he simplified matters and avoided any further talk about alternative judgements open to them. In other words, one clause could send the gang to Australia. The learned judges had ignored the fact that the robbery could not be proved. They had assumed an aim to rob the man after striking him almost unconscious.

With hindsight, it seems amazing that the trial could have led to this result, given the lack of any clear view of the case. It has that flavour of 'showing other crooks the tough arm of the law' given at a time when street assaults and drunkenness were a profound problem for the city. The other relevant factor here is that there

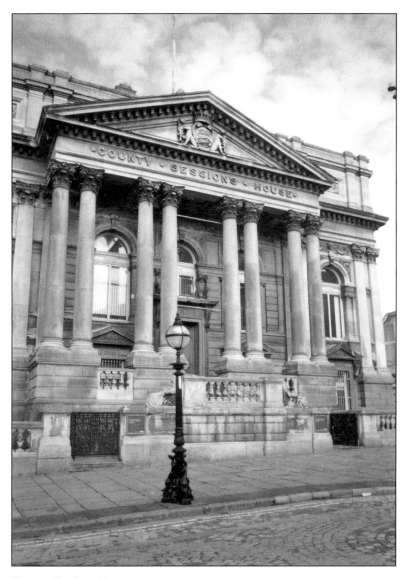

County Sessions House. The author

had been a campaign against transportation for decades before this trial. Only a year after these events, the Penal Servitude Act was to introduce the 'ticket of leave', releasing convicts on leave after a given period of good behaviour. It was in the early fifties that transportation was grinding to a halt. So this conviction was notably draconian and rather against the tide of opinion about punishment. Ironically, within a few years, the ticket of leave initiative was to lead to a widespread belief that a new increase in street robberies was due to that same leniency – the public wanted them all back over the seas, out of the way.

We can only imagine the reactions of the accused as they stood so long in the dock, desperately trying to follow the arguments of the learned men in robes, with the asthmatic Maule coughing through the whole proceedings. But it was not a happy outcome for them. That particular bench wanted to set an example. It was just another street robbery, but this time it went to the Crown Court; the gang of rough miscreants must have been shuddering in their boots. They had picked on the wrong type of victim this time. Worse still for them: they had no lawyer for them with any notable degree of smartness or 'gift of the gab' when the odds were against them.

The context for all this street violence was one of extreme deprivation. In 1847, referring to Manchester, *The Times* reported:

> The streets are crowded with paupers, most of them Irish, who have travelled to Manchester from Liverpool.. in hope of obtaining . . . the public bounty of the town. A soup kitchen has been established . . .

In his novel, *Redburn*, published in 1847, partly set in Liverpool, Herman Melville wrote:

> Of all the sea-ports in the world, Liverpool abounds in all the variety of land-sharks, land-rats, and other vermin which make the hapless mariner their prey.

CHAPTER 5

The Cafferata Poisoning

1860

The finger of guilt points obviously in one direction . . .

In 1854, doing what thousands of people had done in the early nineteenth century, Ann James arrived in Liverpool hoping for a new life in a growing and exciting place: a city with business possibilities perhaps. She found a place in the Vauxhall Road and set about making the property a 'nice little earner'. There was plenty of space, so she let out rooms to lodgers. Then she expanded even further.

The ground floor area became a grocery and restaurant. Business was thriving after a few years, and then what happened was very much in the pattern of immigrant life: her family from her native Devon started to come north and join her.

Her sister had a family; then there was her niece and her husband, a japanner called Cafferata. Success breeds success, and not only did the family become involved in the business, but also a lodger called Tom Winslow: he was a steelworker, but was attracted by the thriving concern he found himself seeing every day; he wanted a piece of it, and before long he was running the retail outlet in the building.

Families generally find it hard to get on when they are living on top of each other, and that began to happen. There was a power struggle, and the sides split into the family people against Winslow. Where could the good, industrious Ann James place herself? Obviously, favouring neither.

That is the foundation of what was to become a complex web of mysterious poisonings under that roof. In 1860, it was not too difficult to use poisons in very subtle and 'legitimate' ways around the house. It all began in January 1860, when Ann James became very poorly. Her attacks of pain and vomiting were regular, and she became worse and worse. With a disgusting lack of sensitivity, taking business acumen to lower levels than one might imagine, Winslow set about trying to ensure that the business would be his if and when the good lady passed away.

The Use of Adulteration, from *Punch*, 1855. Author's collection

Winslow's effrontery and callousness are stunningly crass. Not only did he pester the sick woman into allowing him to take £130 from her bank account, but he tried to have her shares in Gas utilities transferred to him. In this he failed, as this could only really be done if a solicitor was involved and a proper will made. It must have been galling to the Cafferata and Townsend folk to see that Winslow managed to have a will made that would hand the business over to him on Mrs James's death. He would have the stock and the retail premises, and the other members of the household would inherit the domestic areas of the property.

Mrs James had £200 in her gas shares: a very large sum at that time. In the light of the rather hastily made will and of subsequent events, the finger of guilt tends to point fairly obviously in a certain direction. Winslow must have seemed an unlikely suspect though, when Mrs James was feared to be merely clinging on to a very painful life in February, and Mrs Cafferata was sent for (she was in Manchester). The scene in the James house for a few weeks after her return was black and melancholy in the extreme: the woman came home and slept with her aunt, as the older woman wasted away. What was noticed, however, was that Winslow played the perfect nurse, and was always helpful and caring. It seemed to work, as the old lady began to brighten up a little; but a pattern of recovery and relapse began, covering a few months up to May that year.

The family physician, Dr Cameron, was suspicious at the nature of this cycle of illness and recovery; it was fairly typical of poisoning, and he took some food samples away with him, to find that there was antimony there. Action was swift: Mrs James was removed to the Southern Hospital, but it was too late, as she died there on 24 June. Antimony at the time was most easily obtained in tartar emetic. When more than a grain is taken it is rejected, vomited out, and so the person would survive. But when given in repeated small quantities, its effects might be confused with any one of a range of other illnesses. Dr Cameron was very perceptive on this occasion.

It would not take a genius to suspect Winslow, the man who stood to inherit most after Mrs James's death. He was arrested, but he insisted that the Cafferatas were the culprits. But this did him no good and, by 20 August, he was in the dock, accused of wilful murder.

There was considerable evidence against the man; a Mrs Foley testified that he had asked her to buy him antimony 'for the dog', giving her a few pence for this. She was unsuccessful, being refused the poison by the druggist. By 1860, nine years after the Arsenic Act, druggists were taking more care with the retail side of their business, more fearful of being involved in domestic murders. But a boy called Maguire also stated that Winslow had sent him to buy something from a Tithebarn Street chemist, and that on the bottle was printed 'Ant.' The boy even said that he had

The Bluecoats Hospital, one of the many infirmaries of the time.
The author

seen Winslow sprinkling the white powder from that bottle onto bread prepared for the dead woman.

Common sense might have thought that such evidence would condemn the man, but this was not the case at all: it could not be proved that the antimony was given with an intention to kill Mrs James. It may have been intended as a medicine, of course, in tiny doses. The jury were not convinced that there was an intention to kill, in spite of the insurance details and the will being made. Perhaps they saw these measures as sensible 'good business' moves on the part of Winslow. Whatever theory we make, what remains is a mystery. Perhaps the only peculiar aspect of the case, given the enmity of the Cafferatas for Winslow, is that Winslow did not become a victim.

This has to be one of the most puzzling poisoning cases of the nineteenth century.

Usually, there is some kind of helpful documentation if the case reached a certain level of notoriety. In this instance, it is perhaps the sheer number of interested parties under the one roof that complicates the issue.

CHAPTER 6

The Killer Butcher

1862

The prisoner then fell upon her with fury . . .

In 1862 Isabella Tonge was a lady of the streets in Victorian Liverpool, and she had been living with Thomas Edwards for eleven years, when trouble started in earnest between them. Edwards, thirty-two, was a butcher, but Isabella had said to others that he was living from her earnings on 'the game.' As they lived in a house that was strictly Isabella's (the rent in her name) then she had a point. But whatever the truth of his attitudes and life with her, knowing she was a prostitute, the case here is that he had a jealous streak in him.

Liverpool was a rough place at that time: the Statistical Society noted that there was one thief to every 1,500 men, and that there was one committal for every fifty-five people in 1860. In 1866 there were fifty-six highway robberies in the city. When the population was growing rapidly, and work was hard to find, crime became a way of life for many, and prostitution was rife. In that situation, so were the problems that went along with that activity. When a woman brought a client back to her room, it was always risky, but in this case, it was dangerous for poor Isabella.

In November of this year she brought home a man called Sullivan, and he was not a new face, a passing client among many: she had known him earlier in her life. Around this time, not only did she bring Sullivan home, but Isabella went away with him, to a destination unknown to Edwards. He was consumed with violent jealousy. In that state, he became rabidly drunk, knocking back beer and rum in large quantities. When Sullivan and Isabella finally returned, Edwards was ready to fight. He backed down when Sullivan faced him and said that it was none of his business where the two had been. Edwards then sat by the fire and brooded, his rage growing with every second.

Isabella whispered to Sullivan that her man had a knife, and she took Sullivan upstairs, saying that Edwards should go up and stay with him (so the enraged young man could be restrained) while she and a girlfriend went to a lower floor. This happened, as Sullivan was persuasive and firm, but the jealous man had only one thought in him, and he ran down to where Isabella lay, then asked her for money. He said that he would not have her selling her body for him any more. As a contemporary report has it, he then 'fell upon her with fury, and with his knife, stabbed her in nineteen places; two of the wounds penetrated the lungs, from which injuries she shortly afterwards died.'

It didn't take long to take hold of Edwards, and he was soon under arrest. But he blamed the killing on all the drink he had taken. Remorse there certainly was not, though, as he said: 'I have had my revenge, and if she and Sullivan was to die, I'd be glad of it . . . I'll be content to die myself.'

It took the jury a long time to come to a decision, and when they did return a guilty verdict, they added that they would like a recommendation to mercy. The foreman did not explain this, but a reporter at the time considered the thinking behind this to be that the arrival of Sullivan had been a provocation. The judge took the recommendation and said that it would go into the usual system but that Edwards should not 'place any reliance on its taking effect.' The butcher Edwards had used his skills in handling a knife much too well, and on the woman he was supposed to care for. He was hanged in Liverpool on 3 January 1862. There is no record of his final days; one suspects that, as with many cases like this with another partner possibly involved, it would have been a situation of extreme passion, interspersed with ranting and remorse. We have plenty of similar cases on record with these features: only the chaplain and the hangman would know the facts, and our memoirs from these men are few.

CHAPTER 7

Murders in the Mean Streets

1873–74

After a drunken row on Boxing Day, he kicked his wife to death . . .

iverpool in the mid-Victorian years was a place of dark and very mean streets. Even indoors, a defenceless person was not at all safe: there were attacks brought on by drunkenness, as well as by desperation and sheer devilment.

Not long before these years, a man was hanged at Kirkdale Gaol, and his dying statement contains some words which typify much of the domestic and street turmoil of a drink-fused working class community at the time:

> *There is not one but knows that when I had drink I did not know what I was doing. They told me that Tommy McCarty was beating my wife, and they pulled me up by my whiskers . . . But I must suffer.*

This appears to be a crazy mixture of self-defence, rage, drunken violence, and then a murder. Over three years in the mid-seventies of Victoria's reign, there was a steady flow of such horrors. People were living on the edge in the new cities.

In 1873 James Connor, a Londoner, went to a music hall in Liverpool, and after that he started talking to Mary Shears, a ship's steward's wife, and invited her for a drink. She rebuffed him and Connor grew violent. This escalated when two men who were walking on the street saw this struggle: they were called Gaffrey and Metcalfe, and as they walked on Mill Street, they heard Connor shout that the woman had been stealing from him. They intervened, and Connor hit Gaffrey in the face. When the man fought back, Connor stabbed him in the neck, and from the wounds he died. His friend was also cut, but not fatally. Connor was unlucky, as he had William Calcraft as his executioner – a man always likely to make a mess of things.

Calcraft pulled the lever but the rope pinioning Connor in

West Derby Courthouse, where many street muggers and robbers faced their fate. Author's collection

position then snapped. Connor was in agony on the floor, but not dropping to his doom. It took a second attempt to achieve that.

When it comes to sheer heartless and enraged brutality, the annals of crime rarely match the short but revolting tale of Thomas Corrigan and the killing of his mother. He came home drunk one night and went to bed. He was in the habit of bringing his girl home sometimes, to sleep with him under the parents' roof, and they didn't like it. On this fateful night he heard his mother complain about this. It was the small words that ignited a huge murderous passion. He came downstairs and shoved her down, then kicked her. When she tried to go upstairs to bed he threw her down the stairs again. Amazingly, the man's father and others stood and did nothing. They had been too terrified of him. He was also hanged by Calcraft, and one witness said: 'He died hard.'

In a boat-yard in 1875, Wigan man William Worthington lived with his wife and daughter. This was a simple case of a 'domestic', only this time, after police had seen Worthington's wife in a bloody state, staggering on the bank, they told her and her man to get off the street.

The next morning Mrs Worthington was dead, killed on the

"'OW ARE YER? PRETTY BOBBISH, EH?"

boat, beaten to death by a poker. He was hanged with the High Rip Gang killers (see Chapter 8).

Mary Williams found herself in the middle of a street brawl in Bootle in August, 1874. This was in Raleigh Street, and it was a place where Irish and Welsh often clashed. It was a tough place to live, many putting up with cellar habitation, and Mary was one of these unfortunates. She was only thirty, and married, living with other people as well as her husband and children in that slum.

The spark that ignited these terrible events was Mary's violence towards a man called Nicholas Manning, who she thought had hit her earlier as she walked in the street. He denied it, but as he walked past her home one day, she threw a cup at him and said, 'I'll give him a mark he'll carry to his grave.' He walked past her again, perhaps being provocative, and this time she snapped. Mary had a pistol under her apron and she took it out. She shot him in the spine and he fell.

'I've done it and I'll do it again!' she cried. There was soon a crowd around the awful scene. He was carried off, and the woman seemed to be excited and out of control yelling: 'There are one or two more I'll do it to before the night is over!' Then she said, triumphantly: 'I shot him hot with powder and ball.'

Manning died after a fortnight in hospital. Mary Williams, under arrest, had no remorse, saying: 'I did it, and no-one but me . . . It was me shot him, and it's an honour to my country.'

Just to complicate matters, though, Manning died of blood poisoning, and at Williams's trial, a doctor said that blood poisoning was common in overcrowded hospitals. Therefore, was it

The Southern Docks today. The author

murder? Did the young man die from the bullet or from blood-poisoning sustained in Bootle hospital? At the trial, though, it was clear that Mary intended to kill Manning. The verdict was murder, not manslaughter. She was hanged in Liverpool on 31 August. Although the judge had clearly informed the jury that it may have been the case that Mary may have meant to frighten and not to kill, it is clear that her recorded words after the shooting sealed her fate.

Hanged on the same day was the despicable Henry Flanagan – a man who had tried to rape and then murdered his aunt, Mary Flanagan. He had strangled her, using a purse string. Flanagan was hanged just before Mary Williams, and this time the executioner was the skilful and very professional Lincolnshire man, William Marwood.

CHAPTER 8

Brutality to Women

1850–90

A sort of mania for woman-beating has taken possession of the ruffian class . . .

In the early years of Victoria's reign, and into the middle decades of the nineteenth century, Liverpool had a severe problem of widespread poverty. In 1847 the council spent no less than £67,000 on poor relief. Medical inspections of over 14,000 cellars inhabited by families revealed that almost a third of them had stagnant water under the foundations. For many the workhouse was the only way out; for others it was crime. The stresses of long working hours, disease, large families and the struggle for food and reasonably tolerable conditions of life often pushed people to breaking point. Many Irish people had swollen the numbers too, coming over the Irish Sea to escape the terrible famine. The population of the city in 1851 was 376,065. In all too many cases, the nearest and most vulnerable victims of the violence emerging from the overcrowded and desperate living conditions were women.

One of the worst areas of the city for crime was between Dale Street and Whitechapel (at mid-century) but a pamphleteer called Abraham Hume, who lived in a very poor district, noted that the worst type of felon was near the river. He said that the streets around there were 'a terror to a solitary policeman, and into which a respectable person rarely ventures. One street contains very few families who pursue lawful occupations . . .'

A correspondent to *The Times* in 1853, asked why there was such widespread wife-beating. He wrote:

It is obvious that if the women of the humbler classes are not to be reduced to the condition of Indian squaws, some check more effective than we now have must be placed on the savage impulses of their husbands.

A modern, 2006, view of Dale Street. The author

The writer had done some research, and he quoted some recent
cases. He continues:

> *This week a woman complained of her husband, to whom she had*
> *been married for thirty years. He was seen to drag her by the hair*
> *along the garden of their house, to beat her with all his force on the*
> *head and face, and to tear the hair from her head by the handfuls.*

Sadly, such scenes were common in the Liverpool of this period.
Research has shown that reported violence in the last half of the
nineteenth century was very high, and, astounding to report,
police violence against women was high too: forty per cent of the
alleged victims of police violence were women. But the usual tale
in the newspapers was of a man in his drink, out of control,

attacking his wife. The fact that a man was handy with his fists would have been a positive image for him in the community in some places, but when that was turned on women, the situation changes radically.

Take the case of Richard Spencer, a fishmonger. He lived with a woman called Liz Wharton, very much younger than he. In 1872 the business was in trouble and they had to move into private housing in Everton. Things had come to a sorry state, but Liz had no idea how low her man had sunk, and that his depression (as we might see it today) changed his character. She woke up one day to find him talking about a suicide pact. He started beating her around her head. Wisely, she ran off and stayed some time with a friend.

Her return to Spencer before she had checked that he had calmed down was a bad mistake; he was waiting for her, gun in hand, and with a head wound. He shot her, and Liz took three days to die. Spencer was another customer for Calcraft on the gallows. We have no record as to whether or not there were any mistakes this time.

Then we have the cases of sudden rage: Peter Cassidy in Bootle, a man who came home drunk and was out of control arguing with his equally drunken wife. This mild and good-natured man turned into a raging beast and attacked his wife with a mallet and a cleaver. Cassidy was a tinsmith, a useful tradesman to have around, but after this horrible deed, he was destined to be just the fifth customer of the new hangman, Bradford-born James Berry. Berry noted in his diary that he found this 'a difficult case' because he was not sure whether the man warranted pity or blame. The execution was recalled by the new executioner with a sense of reverence and respect for the killer:

> *He walked to the scaffold with a free, firm stride . . . On the scaffold he entered into the Roman Catholic service, which Father Bonte was reading, repeating the responses firmly and fervently. In fact, he was so engrossed in the service that I do not think he knew that I had pinioned his legs. He continued in his prayers as I adjusted the white cap over his eyes . . . .*

The man who had brutally slain his wife now 'blushed crimson to the very roots of his hair' as he left this world.

In 1885, not long before Christmas, George Thomas, a sailor, was enjoying a drink in Toxteth with a lady of the night, one Mary

James Berry, the hangman. Author's collection

Askins. Mary was trying to say goodbye to him and move on, but he would have none of that. He ordered some drinks, and the waiter left to fetch these, when Thomas suddenly pulled a gun and shot Mary in the head. He then tried to do the same to himself, but failed to take his life. He lived to face trial, and then to face James Berry. There was no doubt that this was a tale of wilful murder. The sailor had pawned his possessions the day before, in order to buy the gun. This time, Berry had no notes to make from the scaffold. It was just another day for him, with another killer sent to meet his maker.

In 1879, Tom Johnson, a young man of only twenty, paid a call to a brothel and he took young Eliza Parton upstairs. There was trouble, and Eliza ran downstairs in distress, her face marked after some fight or struggle. But worse was yet to come. Johnson followed her, and he brandished a knife. After stabbing her in the neck, he ran away into the streets. This strong young man, solidly built and tough, was soon in the arms of the law, and in the dock, he collapsed in a fit of weeping when he knew that he was to hang.

It has to be said, to redress the balance a little, that, as Dr John Archer has shown, reported violence by women in Liverpool was twice the national average. He notes that 'North West women had a fearsome reputation for being more violent than anywhere else in the country.' He makes the point that women accounted for over thirty per cent of common assault prosecutions in Liverpool between 1850 and 1914. Maybe, in many cases, they were having to fight back against such a tide of rage and hatred from their menfolk.

CHAPTER 9

The High Rip Gang

1874

My business is taking money off passers-by . . .

J ust a few days after a triple hanging at Kirkdale Gaol in January, 1875, a *Times* journalist wrote a feature on what had become a national concern: 'Crimes of violence.' The writer knew Liverpool, and he told the wider world about the city's problem with 'corner men':

Nobody could shut his eyes to the fact, after what had occurred lately, that there had existed for some time in Liverpool a particular class of persons who had become so well known as to acquire the

Kirkdale Gaol. Liverpool City Records Office

*name of 'Cornermen' whose business it had been to muster at the
corners of streets and commit assaults, with a view to robbing and
plundering unfortunate persons who might happen to pass by. Some
of the recent assaults had resulted in cases of a terrible description.*

The writer was exactly right. Some attacks had ended in murder.
Earlier writers to the papers had clamoured for the use of the lash
against street robbers, even those who were no more than street
urchins.

In August 1874, a gang of these cornermen had been hanging
around, looking for a victim, at the end of Tithe Barn Street. They
were standing beneath a lamp-post. The unfortunate victim that
day was a young doctor, Robert Morgan, who had come to New
Ferry for a shopping trip. As he walked by the gang, John
McGrave, just twenty but an accomplished thug, asked him for
sixpence to buy some beer. McGrave's gang was known as the
High Rip Gang, and they had conducted a campaign of terror in
North Liverpool. McGrave didn't like it when Morgan told him to
'get a job.' That was truly a fatal mistake. The gang set about him,
and knocked him down. 'My job is taking money off passers-by!'
McGrave answered. The basis of their terrifying business was to

Tithe Barn Street today. The author

instil fear and then administer the brutal beating quickly and with sheer force of numbers, overpowering the victim of their hatred.

After that the attack became relentless, brutal and vicious. Michael Mullen, only seventeen years old, joined in with enthusiasm, and soon the two principal assailants were kicking Morgan along the pavement like a football. After a while, police officers arrived, but by that time, the young doctor was dead.

Morgan's brother came after them, and police were close behind. Later that night, the main culprit, McGrave, was apprehended, and the rest of the High Rip villains taken in the next few days. The whole bunch of thugs were teenagers; Mullen had tried to run away to sea. But they were taken into custody and faced a murder charge.

In court, the jury found them guilty of wilful murder, but recommended clemency for a man called Campbell. Justice Mellor indeed passed the death sentence, but Campbell was reprieved a few days later. He had a certain record of good behaviour, and that saved his neck. Even that was no easy task, however, a petition had to be signed, collected and sent to the Home Secretary. But the public sense of outrage was not only in the columns of *The Times*; Liverpool families insisted on the young men being flogged to death, as hanging would have been too sudden and merciful. Obviously, that was not widely supported, and expressed a gut-reaction to the sheer heinous nature of this killing.

McGrave and Mullen were hanged at Kirkdale on 3 January 1875. The violent leader of the High Rip Gang was terrified of the noose. Young Mullen was, apparently, much firmer and resolute in the face of eternity. A reporter at the time noted that a point had to be made about the manner in which these young men had killed their victim:

> *Three executions in one day will excite, it may be hoped, a salutary terror among the roughs, not only of Liverpool, but of the country at large. Of late they have learnt by an inaccurate but not unnatural induction to regard murder by kicking as different in kind from murder done by other means. They have learnt also to regard murders in slow time as different in kind from murders done at a blow . . .*

The 1870s were a particularly busy time for the two Liverpool gaols, Kirkdale and Walton. The latter had started operations in 1854 as a panopticon or radial idea. But the two gaols shared their execution shed for some years, the gallows being taken from one to the other. Kirkdale did not close until 1892. These young cornermen would have found the Kirkdale hospitality markedly stern, miserable and tough.

This particular gang, though, were not finished yet. In September 1877, Thomas Mullen and Mary McGrave, brother and sister of the two hanged men, kicked a man to death, only for the fact that he was trying to intervene in a quarrel involving his wife. Cornermen took a long time to die down, as the finger of blame was pointed at the police, and they eventually scaled up the street patrols. The cornermen episode provides significant evidence of the absolute terror created by youth gangs in an age of packed streets, dark alleys and 'no-go' areas for the bobbies on the beat.

Finger in the Till

1875

He was charged by the jury . . . of embezzling three several sums of money . . .

In the mid nineteenth century, Liverpool was teeming with reformatories and industrial schools. The problem of juvenile delinquency was to be a thorn in the flesh of successive councils, through to the twentieth century, when forward-looking and experimental measures were taken, avoiding the tough regimes of earlier times. But this is a tale of a crime not committed by a young thug, but by a corrupt officer.

In the 1850s, there were reformatories at the Liverpool Reformatory Farm School for boys, Newton; a similar place for girls at Mount Vernon Green; the Clarence reformatory school ship off New Ferry, and Toxteth Park Girls' Reformatory at Park Hill Road. There were frequent riots and revolts at some of these: on the *Clarence*, at the end of the century, the ship was burnt out and the boys housed in premises on Shaw Street.

Even when the juveniles were sent away, often trouble followed. When the *Clarence* was destroyed in 1884 after six boys had started a fire, the boys who didn't stay in the city were sent to Leicestershire, at Whitwick. What was happening was that a series of laws were passed after 1847, to gradually replace prison sentences with work in industrial schools. It was hard work trying to maintain order, as was shown by a clash of boys and staff at Whitwick in 1878, when a gang of boys armed with knives took some of the building's keys; police were called out.

These schools needed administration and staff. The work done there involved positions of trust. Unfortunately, some men were the wrong types for the job. One such character was John Graham, whose case was destined to be heard at the Crown Court. The cash causing the temptation to steal 'from the till' came from parental contributions maintaining their children in reformatories and industrial schools. The Kirkdale Industrial

Schools, for instance, had a governor who was paid £220 in 1854. They were huge concerns. In 1871, Graham (a police constable) started the embezzlement in a modest way, stealing one pound and six shillings. From then onwards, he became more bold, and the thefts more regular.

Graham had started in that position in 1866, recommended and paid by the Watch Committee. He was paid quite well: thirty shillings a week. His contract was clearly expressed: he was 'to act, until further notice, to take proceedings against the parents of children committed to the reformatory and industrial schools . . . for collecting and recovering such contributions on my behalf . . .' This was written by Mr Turner at the treasury. Clearly, the man was held in high esteem when this was first put into practice.

But in 1871 alone he helped himself to a fairly large sum of money (£6) but the point was more about how the authorities could punish him, rather than the sum stolen. After all, here was an officer in a position of trust, doing a despicable thing that would give the Liverpool Police a very bad press, and this at a time when they were being criticised for heavy-handed methods and indeed, for too frequent assaults on the public. The Crown Court appearance was to get their man under the Larceny Act of 1856.

At appeal, it was going to be difficult to sort this out, but Lord Coleridge made it clear that, because Graham was strictly in the employment of the state, as well as in that of the local corporation, he could be charged. His appeal failed, and Graham, as he had been appointed by the inspector of prisons, was sent to be a guest of Her Majesty himself.

The case highlights the problems which came along when cities such as Liverpool tried to find ways to not only keep the young offenders off the streets, but also out of the prisons. Charging the parents meant that it was to be a hard task to make sure they paid up. Graham clearly had some skill in that way, and in modern terms, he obviously had the hardness and sheer presence of a debt-collector. But the temptation was too great. He realised that, if he said that such a parent had not paid (and he had pocketed the money himself) who was to know? He was found out because there were complaints about money paid from the more assertive parents. The Liverpool authorities knew that they could punish him, but it was a question of how severely they could do so.

Meanwhile, the troubles in the reformatories went on: they were prisons under another name, some tended to say. By 1916 there was open discussion in the papers about whipping the young offenders off the streets, and whipping them harder when they were in custody. It didn't help the situation that an officer of the law had worked the system to his advantage. But he didn't get away with it.

CHAPTER 11

A Bomb Outside the Police Station: Fenian Troubles

1880s

The bomb consisted of a piece of iron gas piping . . . filled with explosives and iron nails . . .

When the Prince and Princess of Wales paid a visit to Liverpool, the Lord Mayor for that year said to the Prince: 'You have passed through the portion of Liverpool in which 200,000 Irish people reside.' The Mayor was worried. He had expected serious trouble. But the Prince replied: 'I have not heard a boo or a groan; it has been simply splendid.'

But this was entirely typical of a time in which the idea of a 'Fenian' was a statement about a serious public fear. The word comes from an old Irish word, *fene*, meaning 'the people.' In 1868–78, it had been the fear of Fenian attacks that had led to the London police selecting officers to be drilled in the use of revolvers. By 1868, there were 400 pistols locked away for safety but ready for use in London police stations.

The Mayor and Lord Chief Justice Coleridge, presiding at the assizes, had been very worried about the royal visit. They had good cause to be. Liverpool had been one of the targets of the Fenians, the secret revolutionary society fighting for an independent Irish republic. The Irish Republican Brotherhood had been founded in 1858, and the Fenians had at first been a branch of extremists in America. By 1880 they had expanded, and at that time a certain O'Donovan Rossa was keen to make the Fenians well known for terror by bombing key targets in Britain. Rossa had certainly had experiences which would harden his attitudes to the British: in 1869, when he was in Chatham prison, he had thrown his own urine from his jerry-pot at a warder, and his punishment had been thirty-five days with his hands manacled behind his back. By 1870 he was out again, and contesting the Tipperary seat in a by-election.

The most outrageous bombing by the Fenians had taken place

RECOLLECTIONS

OF A BUSY LIFE

BEING THE

REMINISCENCES

OF A

LIVERPOOL MERCHANT

1840—1910.

BY

SIR WILLIAM B. FORWOOD

D.L. J.P.

ILLUSTRATED WITH SEVENTEEN PLATES

" *Work for some good, be it ever so slowly ;*
" *Cherish some flower, be it ever so lowly ;*
" *Labour ! True labour is noble and holy.*"

LIVERPOOL:

HENRY YOUNG & SONS

1910.

Title-page from the memoirs of Sir William Forwood, 1910.

Author's collection

in Clerkenwell in 1867, when an explosion killed thirteen people; then in Manchester, in the same year, a police van with Fenian prisoners was ambushed and a police sergeant called Brett was shot and killed. Liverpool's turn was to come: obviously, a place with such a massive Irish population would make the authorities nervous. The military were often on the alert in these years.

In March 1881, the British Consul in Philadelphia became aware of a planned bombing campaign in Britain led by Rossa. On 10 April he sent a message home which read: 'I hear from different secret sources that it is contemplated to blow up public buildings in Liverpool.' He even knew what the main designated targets were going to be. Rossa was planning what he called his 'skirmishing' campaign. As a British spy was later to report, some of the schemes were daring in the extreme. They even planned a submarine torpedo boat intended to inflict terrific damage on the British navy.

Then, on 16 May 1881, in the blackness of midnight, an iron pipe-bomb filled with gunpowder was put in the Dale Street police station doorway. Fortunately, the bomb killed no-one and damaged some windows on the ground floor. But worse was to come, and with yet more wild bravado, the Fenians then went for the town hall, and this time there was an element of luck in the fact that the building was not seriously destroyed. A police officer happened to be nearby and he disturbed the bombers. The bomb contained the kind of dynamite used in mining and quarrying, not the little chamber of packed nails. The policeman managed to take the bomb away; his courage was something to wonder at, as after

Liverpool Town Hall, showing the doorways where the bombs were placed. Author's collection

he carried it to a safe position, it exploded soon after he walked away.

There was a chase through the city and the bombers were tracked down and apprehended. But there was a similar attempt later, again with the town hall in mind as target. The Mayor reported that, 'The miscreants, after lighting the fuse, ran away; but thee town hall was watched by a double cordon of police. The first took up the chase, the second joined in.' Those Fenians were sentenced to fourteen years penal servitude. They had also tried to blow up the customs house. At one point in these troubles, the Home Secretary, Sir Willliam Harcourt, asked how many troops might be required to keep the city tightly secured and watched. The regional commander, based in York, wrote to the Mayor saying he would like to send a Gatling gun: 'they are grand things for clearing the streets.'

Later, after the arrests, the Liverpool authorities had been told that in a ship from New York there would be a consignment of thirty-one barrels of cement and that these should be checked. One writer, involved in this, recalled the occasion:

We placed a plain-clothes officer in the Cunard office to arrest whoever might claim the cement, which, however, no one did, and we took charge of the casks as they were landed . . . I was asked to go down to see the machines, and found them lying on a table in the detective office, several police officers being gathered around . . . I

Liverpool Town Hall today. The author

lifted the cover of one.. and immediately the works started in motion, and with equal rapidity the police vanished from the room . . .

These bombs were cleverly constructed: they consisted of the clockworks, parts easy to charge and explode with reasonable precision, and six dynamite cartridges wrapped and placed below that mechanism.

Two years later, in 1883, a man called James McDermott, known as Red Jim, sailed from New York to Liverpool, using the name of Peter Guigley. When he arrived he stayed at the *Railway Hotel* in Birkenhead, but the spy network for Britain had him in its sights and a man called Jenkinson met him and took him to London, remaining in the guise of a Fenian sympathiser. After Red Jim had continued his travels and was being observed, word was spread that he had been behind some of the bombings, with a centre in Cork, and with operations directed at Liverpool. When McDermott returned to Liverpool, on board the SS *City of Montreal*, disguised as Quigley again, he was met on arrival in Liverpool dock and taken off to Walton Gaol. This was not, though, what it seemed.

This had all been a ruse to have a 'plant' in the Fenian ranks; the man was eventually released without trial. It gives us that element of farce so often found in bomb stories and spy stories from that period. Farce and black comedy were never far away in this story. Red Jim had been working for the British secret service for many years, selling his information to the British Consul in New York.

Perhaps the most bizarre tale of the time is that of a morning when an artificial leg crashed through the window of Liverpool town hall. In the panic. Someone asked what had happened, asking if this were a bomb. A calm policeman explained: 'Don't be alarmed . . . it's only an old pensioner's cork leg.' There was a row outside, but no Fenians. The panic came from the fact that the cork leg was just the right size and colour to be mistaken for a gas-pipe bomb.

CHAPTER 12

He Killed Grandma

1883

This is poor work. He is not dead yet . . .

This is a story as much about the hangman as it is about the murderer he was supposed to send to the next world. Henry Dutton, an ironworker, had killed Hannah Henshaw, his wife's grandmother, and was due to be hanged in the precincts of Kirkdale Gaol on 3 December 1883. The problem was that the man charged with seeing him quickly into oblivion was Bartholomew Binns

Binns was only in the office for a year, and was sacked. Later, he assisted the more competent Tommy Scott in 1900, but in his own *annus horribilis* as hangman he was responsible for a few botched jobs. He had helped the very professional and successful William Marwood, from Lincolnshire, who had invented the more humane 'long drop' method which involved more skilful calculations of the drop/body weight ratio. But Binns did not learn much. There were several complaints from governors and clergy about Binns's work and he was politely asked to go. He had a moment of notoriety when he was written about as the man who hanged one of the Phoenix Park murderers, O'Donnell.

But poor Dutton was to be hanged by Binns at Kirkdale. He had hanged a man for the first time just a few weeks before (Henry Powell at Wandsworth) but Duttton was only the second in line for the tyro executioner.

There was a special element of drama in the case, as two local journalists were to be present, and also Dutton had asked the chaplain to give the optional Condemned Sermon on the Sunday before the fatal hour. The sermon was given, covering three warnings that are surely totally irrelevant, if not insulting, to a condemned man: not to be drunk, not to allow a bad temper to possess you, and not to marry in haste. Unless these were likely to happen in the next world, the whole affair appears to be cruelly ironic. But in the very early hours of his last day on earth,

Dutton had something to eat (cocoa, bread and butter) and took sacrament in the prison chapel.

At seven Binns arrived. For some odd reason, the governor would not allow Binns' assistant to enter Kirkdale. It was normal practice to have a hangman together with his assistant. But the prison bell began to toll at a quarter to eight and in haste, Dutton was brought to meet Binns and to be pinioned ready for the drop. Then, as the chaplain read some text concerning man's sins, the ritual walk to the scaffold began.

This final walk was in line with regulations: the chief warder led the way, followed by Dutton and two warders; then Binns was behind them, followed in line by a doctor, the under-sheriff and chaplain. So far so good. But then they reached the scaffold.

The drama came when Dutton was given the rapid final pinioning and strapping ready for the lever to be pulled; the clock for eight had not struck, and Binns walked to look at his victim, causing a rather nervous atmosphere. Dutton asked Lord Jesus to receive his soul. Then the clock struck, and the lever was pulled; Dutton dropped, but it was not a quick death.

The doctor looked down at the struggling man on the rope and said: 'This is poor work, he is not dead yet.' In a drop of almost seven and a half feet, the body spun and the man did not die for eight minutes. That was outrageously cruel by any standards. The doctor could see what the problem was: a very thick rope had been used (like a ship's hawser, the doctor said) and Dutton was very short, only five feet two inches. The result was what every hangman feared: slow strangulation rather than a snapping of the spinal column with speed and humane intention.

There was an inquest after all this farce, Mr Barker, the county coroner, in charge. The prison governor, Major Leggett, made a long statement outlining the time taken for the culprit to die, and also added that nothing had been done to 'hasten the end' of the unfortunate Dutton. The doctor's evidence would make difficult reading for anyone concerned about the terrible suffering the man had experienced: only a slight separation of two bones in the vertebrae near the point of contact with the rope had happened, rather than any sharp break. In the doctor's opinion, the noose had been placed at the wrong position near the nape of the neck, rather than under the jaw or the ear. There was, it was stated, a difference of 300 pounds in weight in the drop/body ratio.

The question that must have been on everyone's lips was boldly asked by the coroner: 'Was the executioner sober?'

Major Leggett answered that he was not sure. Then an

interchange took place, something that must have ensured Binns' departure from his post:

> *Coroner: Has the hangman left the gaol?*
>
> *Leggett: Yes.*
>
> *Coroner: I wish he were here.*

A juryman asked the governor's opinion of the affair. Leggett said: 'I think it was inefficiently performed – clumsily. I did not like his manner of conducting the execution. He seemed, in adjusting the strap on the man, to do it in a very bungling way, which I did not like at all.'

It was one of the most disgraceful cases of a botched execution in the annals of that grim but necessarily professional task at that period. As Shakespeare said in another context: 'If it were done, when 'tis done, 'tis good it were done well.' The coroner considered the affair to have been a disaster, referring to the fact that 'the executioner seemed to be a new hand at the work' and that he should have done what the previous man, Calcraft, had done, that is pull on the legs of any man dangling but not swiftly dying.

One final irony in the Binns story is that he took part in a show featuring ex-hangmen, and that, as one writer of the time said, he 'reveals his art for the entertainment of the large crowds . . .' Incompetence was not to deter Mr Binns from making his year's deadly work the stuff of a media circus.

Chapter 13

Murderous Sisters

1884

This horrible story must be investigated with the greatest speed . . .

There has been life insurance in Britain since 1762 when the Equitable Society started the first business. But there were always problems for the early companies, such as the fraud experienced by the Albion, founded in 1805, and the Eagle, started in 1807. It was only when the actuaries came along, and Milne's Mortality tables were printed in 1815 the way was open for smaller, working class companies to start business in the new rabbit-warren streets of the new industrial towns. The Institute of Actuaries was formed in 1848, and from that point there was always going to be the possibility that persons with a vested interest in a relative's death would break both the law and the moral code.

With that in mind, it is unbelievable how easy two Liverpool sisters found it to take out insurance on their family victims: they were killers, with a fondness for using poison. This murderous habit was to lead them both to the Kirkdale gallows. Their story was a huge media sensation, with a high-profile trial, and even to the creation of their effigies at Madame Tussaud's Chamber of Horrors.

Horrible is the correct adjective to use for what Margaret Higgins and Catherine Flanagan did in 1883. That period

Mrs Flanagan. Andy Tennick

was a busy one for the Liverpool police. In 1884 there were almost 7,000 people arrested in the city for being drunk and disorderly. In the Catholic slums of the north of the city, around Blenheim Street where the sisters lived, the labouring men lived a tough life, and for many it was a short life. That bare fact opens up the potential for types such as these sisters to exploit the life insurance system. So many people died of such illnesses as dysentery or fever that anyone who had been poisoned with arsenic could only really be spotted by a very astute doctor, and the medical men working in those streets would be working long hours and suffering from the stresses and strains of that work.

The tale begins with the women: both daughters of an Irish labourer, and born in Ireland; dates are uncertain but Angela Brabin estimates that Catherine was born around 1829 and Margaret around 1843. Catherine had lived in various houses in this area for over twenty years when she was arrested and interviewed in 1884. Her family was typical of so many working class families in the area: taking in lodgers, frequently moving house, and living a shiftless, vulnerable life in poor conditions. Catherine's family and lodgers consisted of her own son and daughter; a lodger called Jennings and his daughter; Peter Flanagan; another lodger called Rimmer and her sister, the widowed Margaret Thompson.

Catherine was a widow too; her husband John had died a few years before the story begins. He seems to have died of pneumonia but we have to be suspicious, given later events. But we should recall that Catherine was a survivor, managing to exist in reasonable comfort, even doing work as a money-lender, living and dressing well. The younger sister appears to have lost her husband in mysterious circumstances, but all traces of his death have gone. In 1881, she was living with her sister and

Mrs Higgins. Andy Tennick

described as a 'charwoman.' The team was ready to act then, when they set about ending the life of the first victim. There were probably ten known victims, but these are the accounts of the main four victims identified by the researcher Angela Brabin. Thomas Higgins comes first. Thomas, described by the Home

The Queen Insurance Buildings, entrance gate, testimony to the success of the business. The author

Office as 'an Irish hodman of the lowest class', was a lodger with Catherine from around 1882. He came there with his wife and daughter – to 31, New Blenheim Street. They had not been there long when his wife died, and he then married Margaret Flanagan. In November, Flanagan's daughter died. Death was already becoming a regular event in the little world around the sisters.

When the whole group of family and lodgers moved house, this time to Ascot Street, Thomas himself died just after that move. Here was a man who had witnessed the deaths of his wife and daughter, under the roof of these sisters, and he had been approached to have life insurance taken out on his own life. Even when he began to experience the same nasty and painful symptoms that he had seen in his family, he does not seem to have acted. There was plenty of evidence about the nature of his illness and death, mainly from a neighbour, Catherine Manville. She made a statement before the coroner on 14 December 1883.

In this statement, she recalled that both sisters had reported on how ill Higgins was, and that Catherine had been asked to come and see him. Her memory of the sick man was expressed powerfully: 'He was in bed. He seemed to be in great agony. He was facing the wall and moaning and scratching the wall with his fingers of both hands.' She returned later and then: 'The deceased put his hand on his breast and said "Oh if this pain had gone from me . . . " he appeared to me to be very bad and suffering much . . .'

Higgins took a while to die. And there was some discussion in court about some liquid thrown into the fire-back. The issue was whether it contained brandy, or something more sinister. Dr Whitford had come to see the patient; he put the cause down to 'bad drink.' There was the smell of drink on his breath and he did say that he had been on the bottle.

Even when the man lay dying, the sisters and their neighbour discussed insurance. This is where we begin to under-

Mr Aspinall, the coroner. Liverpool City Record Office

No 2 Silvester Court. Liverpool City Record Office

stand the heartless and iniquitous core of this terrible crime. Margaret Higgins was given money by the insurance company after this, and what the sisters did when planning a murder was to try to obtain multiple policies of different kinds; for instance, this one was done under a rule from the British Workmen's Association with a ceiling of £20 (done without a medical). Margaret was the one who performed the grief-stricken wife in this business.

All this meant that sums received on their victims' lives varied considerably. For Thomas they received sums from three companies, totalling £108, though not all of this was paid out. This was a very large sum for a working class family at the time. In court, what became a centre of attention was the ease with which policies could be taken out, and the frequency of policies being approved by senior staff at these small firms.

One fact at the centre of all this was the previous physical robustness and good health of the man who had died; he was known by his peers as 'Crack the whip' and he was very strong. It was Flanagan's brother, Patrick, who played a major role on arousing general suspicion about the death. He asked around at the burial clubs and small insurance firms in the city. It was when Patrick actually brought Dr Whitford with him to see the body that something very underhand was suspected; the man had died from arsenic poisoning, not dysentery.

From that point, the backstory emerges, as other bodies were exhumed. First Mary, Higgins's daughter, was studied by Dr Lowndes, the police surgeon. It was clear from this that despite details about her suffering from pneumonia, the cause of death was probably arsenic poisoning; there was evidence from discolouration in her stomach and from the preservative action of the poison in some organs. There was no evidence of any insurance policy on her, and after interrogations, it was Margaret Higgins who was tried for the murder.

Then came Maggie Jennings, only eighteen years old. This 'strong, healthy girl' as her father described her, started feeling very unwell after eating dinner on 14 January 1883. The poor man heard his daughter vomiting grievously, and it seems that the sisters took over bedside duties and as the father later said, he was 'prevented by Mrs Flanagan' from seeing her. A doctor came to see her – this time a new man called Rafter – and he was confused and not up to doing much except that this was yet another case of pneumonia in Liverpool's unhealthy lodging houses. Once again, the sisters put on the caring and concerned act, seeming to be competent carers and then, when victims were in severe decline, they acted as though they were terribly distraught. This gave medical men like Rafter a certain confidence in leaving these killers alone with the patients, thus ensuring that the sick-bed would become the death-bed.

The last certain victim was from years before, and he was exhumed in January 1884. His body had been in Ford cemetery since December 1880. This was the son of Catherine Flanagan, a young man of twenty-two who had been 'entered into clubs' just a few weeks before he died. The same conclusions came from the examination as had applied to young Maggie: organs well-preserved and no indications of a bronchitic condition which would have caused death (as was on the death certificate). A chemist, Edward Davies, found a great deal of arsenic in the liver. At the time of the death, his mother had put it about that her son had been killed by Catherine Flanagan, and the latter had actually taken out a suit against her for slander. With her usual skill of obtaining cash by not working for it, the killer received £5 from this.

In her confession, Flanagan said that 'My son John followed and he was insured by me but Higgins poisoned him and got a share of the money.'

The trial was sensational, of course, as it brought out a long-standing trade in insurance fraud and downright wilful murder in this community. Questions were asked about the whole business of 'poisoning rings' in such places, and also about the process and probity of the small firms undertaking insurance and burial club work.

The sisters' exit from the world was also big news. One reporter at the time summed up the public feeling: 'The thought that these women had sent their nearest kith and kin into untimely graves after slow agonies of torture by poisoning should, perhaps, have enabled the most sensitive heart to regard their richly deserved fate with indifference.'

Their fate was recounted as graphically as their crimes; Higgins was terrified and heard nothing of the chaplain's supposedly comforting words, whereas her sister 'required little assistance to reach the scaffold.'

CHAPTER 14

Dangerous Deeming, Ripper Suspect

1891

This beast left a trail of bodies behind him, from Merseyside to Hull . . .

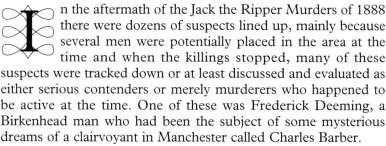n the aftermath of the Jack the Ripper Murders of 1888 there were dozens of suspects lined up, mainly because several men were potentially placed in the area at the time and when the killings stopped, many of these suspects were tracked down or at least discussed and evaluated as either serious contenders or merely murderers who happened to be active at the time. One of these was Frederick Deeming, a Birkenhead man who had been the subject of some mysterious dreams of a clairvoyant in Manchester called Charles Barber.

Barber wrote to Scotland Yard, insisting that he had dreamed of the man who matched the Deeming picture (in most daily papers for some months). Barber had never been to Whitechapel, but was convinced that Deeming had been on the rampage there. The story went sadly wrong when a young woman who said she had walked out with Deeming on two occasions in Whitechapel was shown to be a 'romancer.' But it must have been interesting at the time. Barber dreamed of Deeming boarding a ship called the *Alaska*, and his letters were quite convincing, at least superficially. But as with so many other Ripper theories, this one evaporated.

But the *Liverpool Daily Post*, in October 1891, found another Liverpool connection, reporting that a mysterious stranger in the city had been scrutinised with references to a Merseyside link to Whitechapel by three men in the *Black Swan*, and 'with the assistance of a constable, they conveyed him to Commercial Street police station.' Liverpool, as was the case with most towns and cities across the land, was in the midst of Ripper mythology and moral panic. The paper also was told that a London CID detective had come north to Liverpool in search of a suspect who was 'in possession of a black leather bag.' Whoever this man was (and

Frederick Deeming. Laura Carter

Katie Rounsell. Laura Carter

he was not the Ripper), the *Globe* made much of the story: '. . . certain documents, wearing apparel, cheque books, and prints of an obscene description are said to form the foundation of a most searching inquiry . . .'

Frederick Deeming was in the centre of these various speculations and myths. What was the truth about him and why was he a suspect for some time? Deeming was born in Birkenhead, probably in 1853. He was the youngest of seven children and was the victim of his father's vicious rages, often being beaten. As a child, he was known as 'Mad Fred' and some of the derangement he later showed may be down to the insanity passed on through his father (who killed himself while in a mad frenzy, shut up in a workhouse). But there is also the possibility of a certain religious mania, stemming from his mother's passionate Biblical fundamentalism; he had a bible with him always when he travelled.

Deeming had always been a tearaway and a trouble to his parents, having run away from them on several occasions; and also appears to have worked as a deck-hand on fishing boats. It is easy to blame childhood in this case, but there was something deeply wrong with this man – someone without a sense of self and with no moral scruples. In his reign of terror he had taken no less than thirty-five other names.

He had settled at Dinham Villa, in Rainhill, with his wife, Marie, after rambling and drinking around Merseyside for some time. They had four children, and Deeming killed these as well; he then buried all his victims under the floors. Here was a psychopath with a habit of murder, a man without moral sense and who had a ruthless, brutal depth to his twisted personality. He was to go on and kill many more people before he was finally tracked down. Deeming had made murder the solution to his philandering problems: he had pretended to be an 'army inspector' when he first rented a room at the villa, and had been smitten with the landlady's daughter, Emily. Marie, the wife, had followed him and her fate was sealed.

Later, it was a 'disagreeable smell' from the floor that made people send for the police. Deeming's insane and homicidal obsession was to leave a trail of foul smells of death behind him.

One night, Deeming, having stored some cement and bought a pick-axe, had the floor ready for the macabre burial, and he went stealthily upstairs to cut open his family's throats. It appears that he was fond of entombing his victims, something he learned to do when working as a plumber at Chester Cathedral. Such was the evil of this man that he had a party to celebrate his engagement to his next woman, Emily. The nature of the man was such that he was always on the move, taking assumed names, and leaving death and mayhem behind. He acted a series of roles as he travelled; when leaving Liverpool after these killings, taking Emily with him and eventually heading for Australia, where he played the part of a nobleman, an educated Englishman with a taste for the high life. He also had good looks and could charm women.

This comes out in one of his other escapades: he went to Hull some time before meeting Emily and Marie; there he established another relationship, and that woman was also a victim of his homicidal urges. In Hull he had pretended to be an Australian businessman called Lawson. But his main intention was to travel to Australia with Emily; he had told the family that he was an army officer on leave, and now he explained that he had to go to India. But the destination was to be Melbourne, and he went there with Emily, planning to entomb her as well. The problem was going to be that the earth there was just not suitable for this. It never worked out, but he still killed his wife, now known as Mrs Williams, because that was the name he assumed when arriving in Australia. Police found her body under a hearthstone. Her skull had been smashed by a blunt instrument.

Deeming was arrested there, in Southern Cross, and charged with murder. Some officers reported that in his cell he had claimed he was Jack the Ripper. His defence of insanity was fruitless and he was hanged on 23 May 1892, despite the amazing fact that his defence barrister was a future prime minister of Australia, Alfred Deakin. Over ten thousand people stood outside the prison that day. His last words, in keeping with is mania, were: 'May the Lord receive my spirit.'

The name of Deeming entered popular culture. The strange interest in the man went so far as to cause scientists to dig up his skeleton in order to show that deviants such as he were closer to the apes than to *homo sapiens*. In the Ripper connection, just one detail kept troubling writers and police officers for some time: the girl in London who said that he had taken her out recalled that he had given his name as Lawson, the name Deeming had assumed in Hull.

Maybe his father had been right about Frederick Deeming – that he had a devil in him and would meet 'a bad end' one day.

CHAPTER 15

Margaret Walber: Husband Killer

1894

She decided it would do him good to be locked in a cupboard

In the last two decades of the nineteenth century, the British courts had to start to rethink their attitudes to the defence of provocation when it came to a spouse killing his or her partner. As there was a very important difference in the outcome of manslaughter as opposed to wilful murder (a trip to the scaffold for murder), then some legal brains thought it was about time that judges and juries were better informed about the various causes of marital aggression and violence.

In a celebrated Lincolnshire case of 1891, this issue had been further clouded by the part that heavy drinking played in such violence. In short, was drunkenness a viable plea as a kind of 'temporary insanity'?

In the story of how Margaret Walber came to take the life of her husband, John, these facts are relevant. But it is a very unusual case. Wives killing husbands are highly unusual events in the legal chronicles. Not only did Margaret kill her man: she revelled in tormenting him as well.

The Walbers lived as grocers; they had been married five years when these events happened, and Margaret was fifty-three. John was just two years older, and Margaret's son, John, by a previous marriage, also lived with them. Two lodgers added to the domestic extended family. Both husband and wife liked to take a drink; in fact they liked to drink most of the time. Young John said at the trial that John Walber was 'a quiet man.. although often drunk, he never struck back when she set about him . . .' Margaret clearly took some delight in giving her husband a clout and she wanted him under the thumb.

The last straw came one day when John went to visit a woman he had lived with seventeen years before this. This was Ann Connelly. They had only been together for a few months and it was a long time ago, but that was still a big problem for Margaret.

She came after him, shouted to Annie if he was there in the house, and when told he was, she heard Annie say 'Yes . . . you can take him. I don't want him.' Margaret set about attacking John with ferocity, striking and kicking him, then led him home again.

That was only the beginning of her brutal regime. The couple slept in the top room of the building, and there she decided that it would do him good to be locked in a cupboard. Poor John was locked up for lengthy periods, and neighbours knew what was going on. There was no report to the police, though, and when a friend came visiting Margaret and the subject came up, she said that he was locked up to 'prevent him going to a bad house.' The visitor was told that Margaret would 'take fly-paper to him.' This was a reference to the 'Black Widows' whose poisoning had become a dark legend in the Liverpool streets by this time.

Margaret was seen carrying a chain and padlock upstairs, and the visitor, Mary Vouse, said that she heard movements upstairs, and some shouting. She heard John calling out, 'Murder! I won't go there any more missus.'

The response from Margaret was, 'I'm coming, Duke of York.' The reference is something of a mystery. But there is no mystery in the outcome: Margaret told her visitor, 'He won't leave this house until he's carried downstairs in his coffin.' When she talked about having flypaper in the cellar for him, her son John protested. He was beginning to see the enormity of his mother's actions. 'Don't give that to the poor old man', he said.

After spending many months locked upstairs, in November, John's sister came to visit. She said that John was lying on the bed looking bewildered. It is a bizarre scene to imagine: Margaret explaining her crazy behaviour by saying that if he wasn't shut up in the cupboard he would go to brothels, and the man's sister being genuinely worried about him, saying she would fetch 'a doctor or a priest.' But what may seem superficially like some strange black comedy then became seriously brutal, as Margaret Walber turned nasty and hard in front of the man's sister, saying that he was only shamming and that the sister would fetch nobody: 'It's all a mockery.'

Things escalated one day when – her hatred of Annie Connelly knowing no bounds – Margaret was drinking, and offered to pay a woman a sovereign to smash Connelly's windows. What is important in understanding this woman is that she had been in prison in the past, and it is that period that is so important in understanding her hatred of Connelly as well as of her husband. In her drinking during November, she shouted about that she had 'done time for him'. Then the day came when she went home to find that her son had left.

Her friend later reported that Margaret came downstairs, saying that her son had gone and had taken his money and his violin. Mary Vouse was there again the next morning, and she saw Margaret come down to the shop, saying: 'My son killed John. John's dead. No. I don't think he's dead, there's blood on his face.' But when the two women went upstairs they saw what Mary reported as a 'scene of a bloody struggle', and the body of John Walber propped against a box. The bloodstains told a story of the man being chased or dragged across the room, fighting for his life.

When Mary brought the police, Margaret Walber made her confession: 'I hit him on the head with a chain. My son John had nothing to do with it.' She was tried on 14 March. Her son testified against her. At the moment of the killing, she had been in a drunken frenzy, grabbing the chain to attack the man. The medical words used to explain the death were 'haemorrhage and shock' but the fact is that there were wounds all over the body; there were cuts on his cheek, forearm, and across his nose (the latter injury being very deep). A telling detail is that some of his beard had been cut off. All this suggests a violent attack, with evidence of the cruel streak which had been so evident in the woman for a long time.

There was now a very bad, antagonistic feeling in the air towards the people still left at the grocer's shop, notably Mary. She and her man had to be protected from attack for a while after the trial. But for Margaret it was all over: she was hanged on 2 April 1894 at Liverpool prison. As for the defence of temporary insanity while drunk, it never stood a chance. There had been years of cruelty before this, and plenty of evidence that Walber was a sadist, taking delight in inflicting pain on a weak man in her power.

CHAPTER 16

The Seafarer and the Bookseller

1895

The man standing over him cracked his head with a poker . . .

In the early hours of the morning of 19 February 1895, a teenager staggered into the street outside his home in Redcross Street, his head oozing blood. People walking to work were amazed at the sight, and some stopped to help the boy. This was John Needham, lodger and assistant to a

The dry dock close to Albert Dock. The author

bookseller called Edward Moyse. The poor boy had experienced a night of hell, with a killer loose.

What became a terrible ordeal started the day before as a visit from a former lodger at the house. Mr Moyse had gone out to consider some books for purchase and John was alone in the house, preparing some food for himself when there was a knock at the door. The caller was a seaman who asked after Moyse, and said he would come back later when the old man was back home. He came back at eight, still too early to meet the bookseller, so young John made the man some tea and they chatted. It was a nervous, uneasy atmosphere, although the stranger was amiable enough at times. The problem was that he obviously wanted to know where the bookseller kept his money.

Moyse had a reputation for being tight with his cash; a local miser is always going to be a target for robbery, and young John was used to taking care of things when his master was out. Moyse was also a loner, a private man who kept himself to himself and had no circle of friends. His book stall was on Mann Island, across from George's Dock. He was well-known around the Pier Head, and something of a 'character.' John Needham, alone with the trust and care of the old man's property, must have been very troubled by this young, strongly built man asking after a cash box. The seaman was persistent and menacing, saying: 'It's very funny that he doesn't tell you where his money is for fear he might die.' John simply said that they were not exactly wealthy, selling very few books.

But the seaman made some puzzling remarks about cash. Reading the account today, it suggests that he was distracted and trying to focus on the reason for his presence there. He talked about leaving some sovereigns in keeping there, and then he asked if the old man might let him have sixpence. The only thing that might have allayed young John's fears is that when Moyse finally arrived, he shook hands with the stranger and told John that the man used to be a lodger there. The bookseller asked his assistant to make up a bed for the next night for the man, and said that the seaman would sleep on the sofa for that night.

They retired to sleep. But the next morning, very early, John woke up and was aware that the visitor was stirring. He was saying that he could wake up the old man, and then seemed to be investigating the premises, asking about a man-hole. He was not even fully dressed, but he swung himself up into the man-hole and then came back.

Young John was lying in bed all this time, wondering what was happening. The stranger came back to him and struck him hard

Mann Island today - the bookstall would have been here. The author

on the head. Then the man carried on snooping and searching the place, before coming back to the boy again and this time as John looked up, the man standing over him cracked his head with a poker. Even in terrible agony, John recalled later that the seaman slammed doors, called 'Good morning' as he walked past the old man's room, and then went out.

As John lay in hospital after being helped in the street, the police went to the house, and there they found what John had mumbled that he had seen: the body of Edward Moyse lying in bed, with his head battered. The officers found a scene that made it clear that a desperate struggle had taken place; there was plenty of blood around, and the killer had obviously been searching for a supposed stash of money. All that was found by police was a sum of £8, under the old man's pillow.

The killer had not done a good job on young John; the boy recovered, and he was questioned by the police. What could he remember about this brutal killer? There seemed to be nothing remarkable at first; any passing vagrant hearing rumours of the miser could have done this and then drifted away elsewhere. But John brought to mind something very particular about this killer: his face twitched. There was decent lead, and the community was told about this, and that the police were very keen to find a man in his twenties, possibly a seaman, with a twitch across his face.

A woman came forward, and he was arrested at his father's home in Edgeware Street. He was William Miller, and he was indeed a seafaring man. He was cool under pressure, and came up with an alibi about the blood-covered shirt found in his room. He

Red Cross Street today. Here, the old man lived. The author

was quick to come up with a story that he had done some work at the slaughterhouse in Gill Street. The police took him there to test the alibi, and he confidently took them to a part of the building where he said he had been working just a few weeks before this. As they were in the presence of a pile of carcasses, this seemed to help him tell his tale about doing the work there.

But the foreman present then told the police that no slaughtering had taken place there for several months. Miller was doomed. The final nail in his coffin was of course that John Needham was alive – something that had not been part of the killer's plan. John, from his hospital bed, saw Miller and the police officers coming towards him, along with some other men, to make an identity parade at the foot of the bed. The boy must have been shivering in abject fear as he scanned the line, fixed his stare on Miller, and then saw the man's face twitch, just as it had done on that fatal night in Redcross Street. William Miller had a date with the hangman.

CHAPTER 17

The Maybrick Sensation

1889

It could be said that Florence was a victim of the judge . . .

In the nineteenth century, the ubiquity of fly-papers in the average home was something that could lead from routine habits to a suggestion of heinous foul play. They were a neat way to rid the house of insects, but when they were soaked, for arsenic to be extracted for other uses, there could be trouble. In Battlecrease House, in Aigburth, this was a factor in the puzzling and desperately sad story of Florence Maybrick. To make matters worse for her, she was married to a man who enjoyed taking tiny quantities of poison, for all kinds of reasons.

When that man, James Maybrick, died, the finger of guilt pointed at his wife. The story went on to become not only a famous and controversial case, but a story that has been acquired by the vast library of Jack the Ripper theories, as James was in the habit of visiting London, and his strange personality gave rise to a certain line of enquiry about him.

The story of the Maybricks began when James was on board the liner, *Baltic*, in 1880. There he met young Florence, only eighteen at the time, and Maybrick was forty-two. Florence had been born in Mobile, Alabama; her mother aspired to wealth and status and

Florence Maybrick. Laura Carter

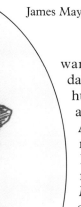

James Maybrick. Laura Carter

wanted the same for her daughter. Mrs Maybrick's third husband had been a German aristocrat, and so the American lady was actually no less than the Baroness von Roques if she wanted to pull rank or put on airs. James Maybrick, along with many other men, found Florence to be very alluring. She was an attractive blonde, blue-eyed and very shapely. It must have been a stunning contrast for her when they married and moved to Liverpool, after living first in Norfolk, Virginia, for a while.

After they married in 1881, they settled at Battlecrease House in Aigburth; the place is a huge building, and Maybrick had acquired considerable wealth in the cotton business. But the change in lifestyle and cultural ambience must have been depressing for the young bride. She was a product of the American South, and of the wealthy, socialising element of that culture. Now she was in a British suburb of a fast-growing industrial city with a very sombre and grey climate. Society and social gatherings were limited for her, and her husband was often away from home.

They had children, and on the surface at least they would have appeared to be like every other middle class couple. But the main problem lay with James. As time went on, his business floundered. Not only was he failing in commerce, but in his personality he was nurturing habits that would ruin his health. Maybrick was drawn to the questionable pleasures of taking poisons and drugs to keep an edge on life (in fact to enhance sexual potency, as arsenic was taken to do). He also lived the fairly typical double life of the Victorian married man: attentive husband at home but mal-contented womaniser when he could find the time and opportunity.

Clearly, Florence would soon find the stress of this relationship, and the loneliness it imposed on her, too much to handle. The fact that Maybrick then set about saving money at home by imposing privations and discipline on the domestic routine was perhaps the last straw. She wrote to her mother (living in Paris at the time) that she was in a mood to leave the house and move elsewhere, and doubted that 'life was worth living', things were so bad. Her situation was ripe for the relief, pleasure and fulfilment that an affair would bring. She found the man in Alfred Brierley, a man in the same line of business as James.

Her mistake, as we look on her life with the knowledge of hindsight, was that she was not discrete. She and Brierley would have times together in London posing as a married couple. But her strains at the hands of Maybrick were intolerable. He had a mistress, and she equally became rash about her attempts to find pleasure outside marriage. There was an element of torment in their relationship, even to the point of Florence flirting with James's brother, Edwin. Things were moving towards some kind of crisis; they were not sleeping together, and Florence was thinking about leaving him.

At this point, enter the fly-papers. Because she was in the habit of using a mixture of arsenic and elderflower to treat boils on her face, the soaking papers were a common sight in the house. But then came James's illness. On 27 April, he was ill and he blamed this on a prescription of strychnine being wrongly calculated. This would have made sense of a man with those strange habits of pleasure. But his health began to decline more severely. Fate was stacking the odds against Florence, as the servants were noticing the soaking fly-papers and linking that to their master's decline. After all, he had cut her from his will and had been insulting and aggressive towards her on many occasions. She had cause to detest him. The illness dragged on, and a nurse was employed to be with the patient at all times.

Maybrick's brother, Edwin, also came, and he took charge of things. The situation then was that Florence was estranged from her man; she was seen as potentially a deranged woman with a grudge against her husband, and there was evidence mounting against her with regard to the arsenic. Even worse, bearing in mind the morality of the time, she wrote to her lover, Brierley, trying to arrange a meeting with him before he left the country; in that letter she referred to Maybrick's condition and noted that he had no suspicion of the affair. Florence was often present at the sick man's bedside and unfortunately for her, she played a part in using the medicines, saying that James had actually asked her to give him some arsenic in powder form. Everything she seemed to do in the role of nurse or caring wife turned into facts to be used against her when Maybrick died, as he did on 11 of May. She was arrested on suspicion of wilful murder, by Superintendent Bryning.

The high drama continued even to the point of her mother entering the scene, there was a confrontation and argument, and Florence put the situation very neatly, saying to her: 'They think

Cartoon campaigning for Maybrick's release. Clifford Elmer Books

Sir Charles Russell. Laura Carter

I poisoned Jim.' She was taken first to Lark Lane station, and then to Walton Gaol.

The trial began at St George's Hall on 31 July, and Sir Charles Russell led her defence. There was great confusion in the forensic and medical evidence, even to the point of two experts disagreeing about whether or not the deceased had died from arsenical poisoning. Events went against her, and in the end it could be said that Florence was a victim of the judge. This is because there was just so much testimony about Maybrick's habits of pumping his body full of drugs and poisons that he was dicing with death, anyway, and ruining his health for many years before these suspicions were first aroused about his wife's alleged designs on him. The judge, Mr Justice Fitzjames Stephen, directed his long summing-up to the likely guilt of Florence if certain facts were ignored: that is, he reinforced the accusations of moral lapses against her, to the detriment of the actual issue of murder. He was ludicrously biased in his dramatic account of the situation of slow poison on a supposed 'loved one.' Naturally, the jury would begin to turn against Florence and forget the contradictions about the actual nature and administering of the poison. Arguably, the judge's action which had the most impact on the jury was his mention of the letter to Brierley about Maybrick being 'sick unto death' and his very evident repugnance at what he was implying she had done and written with such callousness. The jury surely must have been influenced by seeing this. There was definitely 'reasonable doubt' in the case, and a death sentence was outrageous. Yet, on 7 August, Florence Maybrick was sentenced to hang. The judge, leaving the court, was the target of general public abuse and displeasure, so wrong was his sentence perceived to be.

The real heart of this sensational trial was Florence's loud assertion that she was innocent of this crime: 'I was guilty of intimacy with Mr Brierley, but I am not guilty of this crime.'

But the real sensation was yet to come; after the death sentence was passed on her. There was a strong and widespread campaign for clemency, and this was going on even at the time that Florence was waiting her fate in Walton prison (with gallows being made ready outside). The Home Secretary arranged a reprieve: the sentence was to be commuted to penal servitude for life. But in 1904 she was released and returned to America. There, as Richard Whittington-Egan has written, she hid herself away in the Berkshire foothills; she became 'Florence Chandler' in South Kent, Connecticut. The person who became the epitome of the dotty and lonely old spinster, surrounded by cats, as Whittington-Egan says, 'was known to successive generations of South Kent boys as *The Cat Woman*.' She died in 1941, aged eighty-one. History tells of two Florence Maybricks, then, but there is another – the lonely prisoner, unjustly incarcerated, in those silent years before release.

History has leaned to the view that gastroenteritis, not murder, led to Maybrick's death.

Chapter 18

Mysterious Death
of a Street Singer

1899

The body was very thin and emaciated . . . covered in vermin

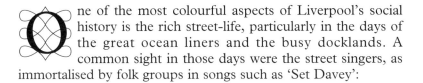ne of the most colourful aspects of Liverpool's social history is the rich street-life, particularly in the days of the great ocean liners and the busy docklands. A common sight in those days were the street singers, as immortalised by folk groups in songs such as 'Set Davey':

Come day, go day, wish in me heart it was Sunday, drinking buttermilk all the week, but it's whisky on a Sunday.

The words of the song suggest extreme poverty and desperation, and most of these people were in that category. The vicar, Francis Kilvert, met such a young girl on the train from Wrexham to Liverpool in 1870, and he left an interesting account of these artists' charms and habits of work:

This girl kept her companion and the whole carriage laughing from Wrexham to Chester with her merriment, laughter and songs and her antics with a doll dressed as a boy . . . She had a magnificent voice and sung to a popular comic air while the doll danced wildly . . .

The girl sang *Dolly Varden* and then, when she left the carriage, she collected money for some bags of peanuts. Kilvert was smitten with her and felt mesmerised. As Henry Mayhew showed in his monumental study of Victorian street life among the poor in London, *London Labour and the London Poor* (1861–62), the street entertainers had a very tough life. He describes such types as street clowns, street bands and conjurors and the physical features described paint quite another picture from that in Kilvert: 'He was a melancholy looking man, with the sunken eyes and other characteristics of semi-starvation.' Some street singers were surely

Remains of the workhouse, Brownlow Hill, where many of the street beggers would end up. The author

lively and attractive like the girl in the railway carriage, but they seem to have been in a minority.

Many of these girl street singers did not laugh so often. Most of the time their life was miserable and they lived in poverty. Such a one was a girl known as Annie Smith, and this poor girl's corpse was found in a house in Christian Street in January 1899, by Sarah Evans, a dock-labourer's wife, and one of her friends, Agnes Watts, had to identify the body. At the coroner's inquest on 21 January, a very sad tale evolved. The place where she was found was very lowly indeed. The officer who first went to see the body recalled that the door was always open and the place had been lived in by tramps for several months, as one of the few dilapidated places where they could put their heads down for a night.

Singers such as Agnes and Annie were often on the road, looking for work and audiences, wherever there were gatherings. Annie was known as a 'steady woman who had never been seen the worse for drink.' She was thirty-one years old and regarded as 'quiet and low spirited.' This is certainly the down side of the image Kilvert gives us.

Annie was new to Liverpool, and it seems that she was based in Manchester. But early in January, Agnes had seen her singing near St Patrick's Chapel. Agnes had known the dead girl for a year and a half, but only in Manchester, never in Liverpool until then. At Princes Dock mortuary, Agnes saw a horrific sight on the slab: the singer was in a terrible condition; she had been found naked, with dirt and vermin on her, and was also emaciated. Perhaps most suspicious was the fact that, as the *Liverpool Mercury* reported: 'The right arm and right side of the body were scarified or scraped for nearly the whole length. The left arm below the shoulder was black and discoloured. There were no traces of injury to the vital organs.' As there were no marks suggesting violence to her head and face, there was no definite evidence that she had been attacked. She may have fallen from a staircase or landing.

The Trials Hotel, off Castle Street, remains of the police court area. The author

The coroner, T E Sampson, at the Dale Street enquiry, insisted that there was no certainty that the body was that of Annie Smith, in spite of Agnes's testimony. He directed some officers to go to Manchester to collect details of the woman's life there. After one previous visit to Manchester, Detective Duckworth had gathered some information: he had found that Agnes (who only had one eye and was therefore memorable) was known by the fraternity of street entertainers, but that no-one said they knew Annie, from the description given. All Duckworth could say was that describing the dead woman as 'a Jewess' was the only way to convey her features.

All this seems to indicate that the girl had died in suspicious circumstances, and one telling detail is that a man called Horace Dunnett, who lived in Spring Place, stated that he had heard a voice shouting: 'Murder!' and 'Police!' from an empty house in that area. As the journalist on the *Mercury* reported though: '. . . such cries are frequently heard in the neighbourhood and little importance is taken of them..' He goes on to give a horrific statement about the lifestyles of the labouring classes of that part of the city at the time:

'. . . it was a neighbourhood in which many drunken women were thrashed by their husbands.'

Whether Annie Smith was indeed the person Agnes said she was, or some other unfortunate, it doesn't matter. What matters is that the evidence points towards some foul play – she was naked and had been dumped in a hovel; she was also starved and had most likely been attacked with some kind of weapon. But she was just one of many, a statistic at a time of frequent deaths among the street urchins and homeless wanderers. The interest in the story lies in what it tells us about the city at the time, and what horrendous problems it was having, trying to cope with the expanding population and with coping with the poor, who of course, are 'always with us.'

The social history behind this story makes it clear that the travelling poor in the county of Lancashire and throughout the North West at that time were often 'on a circuit' looking for places where word had got around that crowds were receptive and the wealthier classes were, maybe, a little more generous than elsewhere. The Manchester travellers were expected to know the Liverpool counterparts, and so on. This tendency for individuals to drift from town to town, just like the girls on the train who met Kilvert, could entertain and even entrance; but the tale of Annie Smith highlights the dark story behind this often popular culture of street singers.

CHAPTER 19

Goudie: Victim and Swindler

1901

Forged cheques were written and then entered in the ledger . . .

In a short but dramatic film narrative in the recently discovered archive of two photographers of the Edwardian era, we see a man in a long black overcoat being escorted by two detectives to Bootle police station. In the grainy, crackling old film, as the commentator notes, we have the first true crime story on camera. Part of the sequence shows headlines from Liverpool newspapers, conveying the startling news that Goudie has been arrested. The film is from *The Lost World of Mitchell and Kenyon*, and in this we can see glimpses of a Liverpool long lost under the bricks and mortar of time. But the images linger: Goudie taken from his lodging house in Berry Street; children gathering, aware that some kind of celebrity has been among them. Not only was the story of Goudie the swindler the first true crime story – it ranks as one of the top three Liverpool crime tales of all time, one could argue, almost as sensational as the Wallace case and the Fenians bombings.

What that film does not tell the viewer is that this man's activities would lead to a high-scale criminal trial at the Old Bailey in which the legal career of that great Liverpudlian F E Smith (Lord Birkenhead) would

F E Smith. Andy Tennick

be launched, and that the future Lord Chief Justice of England, Rufus Isaacs, would also be involved in the case.

Who was this man of mystery? Amazingly, he was not a major-league criminal whose name would cause hearts to stir and doors to be locked at night. He was just a poor ledger clerk with the Bank of Liverpool. His time was spent filling in accounts books and sharpening pencils. He might have passed his life that way, in obscurity, except for one character trait: a liking for a flutter on the horses.

Thomas Peterson Goudie was from the Shetland Isles. He lived a life of routine in the city, staying in a lodging house for just £1 a week. In 1900 he would have seemed a quiet man, respected for regularity and hard work in the office. He was twenty-nine and well-educated; his wage was reasonably good for the time at £3 a week. But since the mid 1890s, he had been betting and losing increasingly large sums of money. By 1898 he was in so much debt from his gambling that he worked out a simple way to defraud his employers of £100. He did this by exploiting a rich man – Hudson, who owned Hudson's Soap, and forging cheques supposedly paid out by this victim. Goudie handled the names between H and K and Hudson was his wealthiest client. Forged cheques were written and entered in the ledger, then destroyed. As Goudie helped with the audits (done weekly) he could soon cover up this crime.

But he kept on gambling and he visited race courses. After a day at Newmarket races in 1900 he met with some touts and cheap crooks called Kelly and Stiles. It was amazingly crass and stupid of Goudie, but he somehow felt that he would tell these men of his scam. That was his fatal move. They realised they had a goose that would lay them golden eggs. Goudie was so simple that he was fooled into thinking they were high-class bookies and that he could have tips from them. As they had something on him, they could force him to bet (and thus simply put money in their pockets) and pressure him, with threats, to increase the level of his embezzlement from his employers.

As matters escalated and word about this source of easy money circulated in the London criminal fraternity, two more characters entered the story. These were two blackmailers called Burg and Mances. Mances was the strong man, the 'frightener' in the racket, and he would travel to Liverpool to threaten him and bully him into involvement with their gang. Goudie had already put the massive sum of £70,000 by way of Kelly and Stiles; now everyone was greedy.

In October 1901, Goudie was found out. In just a few weeks,

the greed of the criminal gang around him meant that he had stolen £90,000 for them. Goudie was cornered and when officers arrived to quiz him, he confessed, but after going to fetch ledgers, he absconded and went to hide away in the Berry Street lodgings. Markes and Mances managed to disappear into Europe (Marks may even have committed suicide) but Goudie, Kelly, Stiles and Burge were charged and all was set up for the major trial at the Old Bailey.

Goudie was tracked down to his lodgings, and the barristers

Rufus Isaacs. Author's collection

gathered for the fray. The judge was Mr Justice Bigham; Goudie's defence was led by F E Smith and Rufus Isaacs appeared for Kelly. On the face of things, Goudie had no chance of acquittal. F E Smith knew that his only chance of any success was to appeal to the jury's sense of the sadness of a poor man duped by a group of evil professional criminals. After all, Goudie was facing penal servitude for life. Smith could at best hope for a shorter sentence. The clerk pleaded guilty and he was put in the box as witness against the crooks from the racing world. Perhaps the most stunning fact in all this is that Goudie himself only received £750. The touts and blackmailers had enjoyed five-figure sums from Goudie's forging habits.

Rufus Isaacs and Marshall Hall, defending the two blackmailers, put their heads together and achieved something that Rumpole of the Bailey would have been proud of: they made it seem right that their two clients pleaded to lesser charges rather than plead not guilty. The outcome would then, if Goudie were guilty (and that was certain) be a short sentence, much less than the anticipated ten year one. They were right. Goudie was guilty, and F E Smith's speech did indeed move the jury. Smith painted a picture a pathetic little man who had been duped by ruthless hard men and leeches who bled him dry. What the jury were asked to see in the dock was not a nasty, unscrupulous conman, but a wreck, a man broken by the harrowing experience of meeting with this tough gang. There was the added factor that Goudie had three sisters, and these ladies had been working hard for their brother, to find some kind of legal aid for him.

Even Justice Bigham could not ignore all this; he passed a sentence of ten years, rather than the expected one of fifteen years. There was a story that F E Smith was so talented and persuasive in this speech that Sir Richard Muir passed him a note which said: 'You will be the master of all of us. No one I have ever heard has impressed me in so hopeless a case.'

But there is a sad irony in the outcome, for Goudie died six years later, in gaol of course. But this incredible story has all kinds of interesting sidelights: the villain Burge, who served in effect only three years, partially redeemed himself by saving the life of a prison warder showing 'conspicuous gallantry.' F E Smith, who launched his career on the case, and it emerges that his wonderful speech was in fact practised and rehearsed to perfection and the whole piece memorised word for word.

As F W Ashley has commented, the Goudie case attracted as much attention at the time 'as a front-page murder.' For a man who had first yielded to the temptations of gambling on the horses, with £1 bets being typical of his risk, to rise to the level of major and notorious national crook was an unmissable story for the journalists. In Mitchell and Kenyon's film, the actor playing Goudie, escorted to the cell by two plain clothes detectives, comes across as someone as dangerous as Baby Face Nelson or Al Capone. Ironically, in a twisted way, his dreams of success and fame, well away from his dull life of pen pushing, came true. The quiet, regular clerk had become the dramatic subject of the sensational *Police News* and the penny dreadful comics. When he had first run away and lain low for a while, the central police office in Liverpool had issued posters with an image of him and a £250 reward. *The Times* gave the story massive column space; they told the tale of Mrs Harding, Goudie's landlady, shopping him to the Bootle police. Her husband, Charles who was a crane-man on the docks, advised his wife to go to the police.

From the moment Mrs Harding stepped into the central police station, the man staying with her, under the name of Johnson, was about to become a celebrity.

It hardly seems the material of gangland or of high tension crime – a quiet little penpusher escorted to gaol by two police officers, taken from a redbrick terrace house in Bootle just over a few streets to the station. But in some ways, the fraud involved in one crook taking on a huge national bank has a media interest perhaps more sensational than a daylight robbery or even a mundane domestic murder.

CHAPTER 20

A Shooting in Great Newton Street

1904

It was a case of rabid jealousy, and he had a revolver in his hand

On 26 February 1904, Mary Pike had an unwelcome visitor at her home in Great Newton Street. This was thirty-nine year old William Kirwan, a sailor. He was Mary's brother-in-law and he was in a savage mood that day. His wife was there with her sister and William raged at her, saying that she had been sleeping with another man, and in that very house. Both sisters insisted that there was nothing going on and that the man's suspicions were totally unfounded. But he had gone there in a foul mood, and he was ready to fire a gun.

Kirwan had it in his head that the two women were using the house as a brothel; what led him to those suspicious thoughts is not clear. But he was so deranged on this occasion that the slenderest scrap of suspicion would enrage him. We know nothing about the origin of all this: jealousy has its own inner language, its grammar of hatred and irrationality – the green-eyed goddess who drives men to kill the objects of their affection.

It was a case of rabid jealousy, and he had a revolver in his hand; Kirwan fired four shots, two at each woman. A man called Russell (a lodger) was the hero of the hour; he dashed in to find Kirwan dazed, gun in hand, pointing the barrel upstairs. Somehow, Russell managed to take Kirwan's wife and children outside to temporary safety in the cellar, and again went back for Mrs Pike, taking her down there as well.

Russell had now gone down to join the women and children in the cellar and he opened a window and started shouting for a policeman.

At that point, Kirwan had reloaded the gun. What happened next was like a scene from some border town in the wild west. The madman got up from the doorstep and fired shots in the air. The street must have cleared in seconds. After that he stood across the road from the house, as if waiting for act two of the drama. But as so often happens in acts of distraction like this, when a police constable approached to arrest him, the man gave in. But here we have the tragic turn of events that also tends to happen whenever guns are involved; Mrs Pike emerged into the street and pointed across at Kirwan, saying, 'That is the man!' She had walked towards them, and the police officer had not yet managed to disarm Kirwan, who had one hand in a pocket. When he saw Mrs Pike coming close he pulled the gun and fired at her from very close. She collapsed, mortally wounded. We know very little about the victim; even her age is unknown.

The policeman completed the arrest and restraint, and at that moment Kirwan said to him: 'I intended to kill the both of them. I'm sorry I didn't. I meant it well enough.' The revolver was taken from him very easily.

Later when charged with murder, he said: 'I was driven to it with great provocation.' It took a few days for Mrs Pike to die, so of course the charge was wilful murder and Kirwan was sentenced to hang. It must have been one of the jury and judge's easiest decisions. There was hardly any doubt in the matter. He had killed the woman right in front of the officer arresting him. Mr Justice Bucknill put on the black cap, as he would do again just one day later for Ping Lun who shot his friend in Frederick Street.

His appointment with death was at Walton Gaol on 31 May 1904, was in the hands of executioner William Billington, with

Guns were easy to buy: advert from 1902. Author's collection

Henry Pierrepoint in attendance as assistant. Billington had really had to prove his professional mettle as a hangman just three years before, when he hanged three women within a year – Emily Swan at Leeds, for the murder of her boyfriend, and two women for baby-farming at Newgate: Annie Walters and Amelia Sach. The Billington dynasty were impressively skilful. A journalist, Patrick Watson, met William and called him 'an excellent workman' who 'gave the most perfect satisfaction to his clients.' A man of many quirks, Billington called the guillotine the 'gelatin.' He was to become well acquainted with Liverpool in the first years of the twentieth century, first as assistant and then as hangman proper.

Chapter 21

Spring-Heeled Jack in Everton

1904

Someone was yelling, in panic, that Spring-Heeled Jack was in Shaw Street . . .

In 1938, a Lincoln man called Rollins wrote to the local paper to tell the readers that Spring-Heeled Jack had been in Lincoln. He wrote: 'In 1877 I lived at a farm in Newport . . . In that winter Spring-Heeled Jack came to Lincoln and jumped over Newport Arch . . . the young men of the town used to come out and try to catch him . . .'

This mysterious street prowler had been supposedly seen in England's streets since the autumn of 1837 when he appeared in London. Most accounts of this rogue who used to assault people at night agree that he wore a black cape and a bat-like cap. He was supposed to have had springs in his shoes, enabling him to jump twenty feet in the air.

A witness in Old Ford, near London, in 1838, said that Jack appeared in the dark street and asked for a light before shoving and robbing the man. Often, he used claws on his fingers to tear clothes before robbing victims. One alleged victim, Lucy Scales, was said to have had flames spat at her by him. All through the nineteenth century he appeared in all kinds of places, so the legend goes. Some of the appearances were closer to what we now call 'happy slapping' than anything else. So powerful was this mythic figure in the popular imagination that, in 1888 when Jack the Ripper was about in Whitechapel, some thought both Jacks were one and the same.

In 1904 he appeared in Everton. First he was seen leaping from the top of the High Park Street reservoir; then witnesses said they had spotted him jumping over garden walls, notably in St Michael's in the Hamlet. Around 1950, when Liverpool writer Richard Whittington-Egan was researching the phenomenon, an old man told him how, in 1888, he had had a sighting. He said he was playing with some friends at St Francis Xavier's Boys' Guild when someone came in, excited, someone yelling in panic that

Spring-Heeled Jack was in Shaw Street. The tale continues, as Whittington-Egan tells it: 'When, however, they reached Shaw Street, they saw no sign of the weird creature, although the exited crowd told them that he was crouched on top of a nearby steeple.' Many said that he had been running across the Liverpool rooftops.

A Mrs Hudson in that same street (William Henry Street) told reporters that she had seen a large shadow on her wall, caused by someone or something outside her window. When she investigated, with some bravery, she said that she saw what she thought was a giant bat on the street-corner. Strangely, the form appeared at the same time the next night. One might think that Mrs Hudson would have left the house gingerly by the back door; but no, she was ready to observe and even to follow. She stated that she ran out to see a figure running down her street, and that it had a dark cloak and wore high boots. When it moved, it did so in leaps. Many of the people in the street had seen the same thing.

Later that week, some groups of young girls reported that they,

Spring-heeled Jack. Laura Carter

too, had seen the figure. It seems ludicrous to report, but even in daylight he appeared, and was seen to leap twenty-five feet in the air. Over a hundred people said they saw him.

He was then reportedly seen almost everywhere, such is the power of hysteria. Or is it simply that? Most of the above accounts might seem whimsical, but the truth is that if the original Jack, abroad in London, was indeed the villain in the experience of Maria Davis in 1845, then the myth is no laughing matter – and not always a myth. Maria was grabbed by the figure and thrown to her death in quicksand.

There are theories about Jack in abundance; many think he was originally the Marquis of Waterford, because of a sighting of the family crest on the black cape, a 'W' in the exact shape of that family design. The expert on the subject, thriller writer and historian Peter Haining, thinks that Jack was created by Waterford and his cronies as a prank, partly to express his anti-female feelings, and partly to trouble the police (who were quite new figures at the time, on the London streets).

Whatever the truth might be, the fact is that hundreds of people swore they saw him in 1904 in Liverpool streets. Mass hysteria? It could be. But sometimes folklore crosses over into criminal records and sometimes the fear caused by rumour and urban myths can be as harmful as a more orthodox and familiar crime. To modern eyes, the whole story seems relatively harmless, but in his first appearances, there was nothing funny about night-time assaults. If the Liverpool Jack was a harmless eccentric who had read about the original London character, then he was still terrorising lonely old ladies: that's the bottom line, and it's dangerous and very fearful to contemplate anything else.

CHAPTER 22

The Madge Kirby Mystery

1904

The probable killer wrote taunting letters to the police . . .

This is a story with a dark and familiar scenario: children out alone, prey to psychopathic predators. We still read stories like this far too regularly in the daily papers. The most we can hope for is some kind of closure, but in this mystery, nothing was resolved and the probable killer wrote taunting letters to the police.

Little Margaret Kirby lived with her sister and father in Romilly Street in January 1908. Her mother had died just a few weeks before this very sad new year began. She was blue-eyed and with brown hair. On this fateful day she was wearing a black shirt and blue pinafore, and with a velvet bonnet and black stockings and boots. Madge and her friend Annie McGovern went out to play and as they walked in Farnworth Street a man approached and offered to buy them sweets. Little Madge accepted and went with the stranger. She was seen on several occasions after that; most clearly by Robert Woodside, who was working in a shop and saw her walking with the man. He had heard the news that she was missing and followed the pair, after calling out to her: 'Come on Madge.' This was while he was delivering goods to a house on Rupert Hill.

As Robert moved towards them and called out, the man restrained Madge and pulled her back to him. Robert made it to just three yards from them, but then the man chased him, and it seems that little Madge was so petrified that she stayed by some railings and made no attempt to escape. Robert did all the right things: he told his father and then went to the Bridewell at Prescot Street to let the law know what he had seen.

Months passed by and spring changed to summer. Then, on 15 August, the worst fears of family and police were realised when a girl's body was found in a sack in Great Newton Street. A workman had seen it and cut it open. He must have been shocked when he found a decaying corpse inside – the body of a child almost naked. It seems as though the sack had only just been moved, prior to demolition work. It had been in a cellar for a long time, and advanced forensics would have made progress in the investigation quite swift, as there were handprints in the dust on the door-jamb. The report in the newspaper at the time said that these were being photographed, but nothing came of this.

Poor David Kirby, only a young man, had to take that terrible journey to identify the body at Princes Dock mortuary. He recognised her clothes immediately, but her body was in such a deteriorated condition that he could not be sure about that. The man was emotionally wrecked. He had to state that he was satisfied that what he had seen was his daughter. There was clearly a great deal of sympathy for the man, including that from Mr Sampson, the coroner.

After so long and after a long and fruitless search for her,

London Road today. The author

Madge Kirby was buried at the Catholic cemetery. Large crowds of people came out to pay their respects and give support to the broken young man. But there was to be such horror still to come, as a letter from a man who claimed to be her killer arrived at the police station. The *Weekly Mercury* took up the tale with a reproduction of the letter: something with a tone very much like the Ripper letters and later, the Wearside Jack letters. The tone and content was meant to provoke and display some perverted egoism. Part of it reads: 'I should like to throw a little light on the murder of my victim, Madge Kirby. Some years ago I was a lodger at 15 Great Newton Street so that I knew the house thoroughly. I am still in possession of a key to the front door . . .'

Mount Pleasant, centre of the area where the street attacks took place. The author

He talks about taking her out for a day's entertainment and then killing her. The writer actually provides 'a real clue' in saying that he was a regular at a certain public house. He ends with: 'I have given you a chance for your money now, so do your best, but I am sure your manhunt will be in vain . . .' There was indeed a manhunt, with bloodhounds, and the chase led from the Botanic Gardens to Lime Street station, where the dog, Czar, stared towards the railway route to the Midlands.

There was then a second inquest and the facts were examined again. Sergeant Blenkhorn provided some photographs and little Annie McGowan was questioned, telling the same story, that the man took Madge by the hands, and that Annie had refused to go with him. Another small boy saw the man and heard him ask the question; he had even waited in vain for Madge to come back. Masses of details then began to emerge, even to the fact that she had been seen in some cocoa rooms on Brownlow Hill. Janes Hughes said that she saw a little girl and man and that the girl was distraught; she was given tea and a cake. A number of other people came forward with reports of sightings.

What emerged was a picture of a mysterious man loitering in Pembroke Court; several people saw him, and one even noticed him climb over a roof. To add to the general air of menace and dark murderous intent by this man still free on the Liverpool streets, a witness said he had seen a man dressed as a woman at 13 Brownlow Street.

At the conclusion of the inquest, Dr Nathan Raw was sure that Madge's death was not from natural causes; she had been killed. A verdict of wilful murder by person or persons unknown was given.

The melancholy coda to the story is that Madge's father, David, died just two weeks after the second inquest. He was just thirty-eight, and had suffered such major trauma that he lost the will to live; he took to his bed. He had spoken again at the inquest, then after telling his sister that 'This has finished me' he went to what would become his death-bed. Romilly Street was packed with mourners on 3 October.

We have to feel a sense of relief and of black irony in the fact that, just a few weeks after this, the probably deranged murderer (if he was so) wrote again to the Liverpool police, this time from Dewsbury, West Yorkshire. On a letter adorned with the skull and crossbones and what the *Mercury* called 'a rude drawing of a child's face', the 'freak letter' invited the law to catch him: 'I dress in black and brown boots and cross the market every day at one o'clock.'

As David Canter has written in his study of profiling, 'In order to decipher a criminal's actions we need to know what narrative he is drawing upon.' In this case, the narrative was clearly one of notoriety and attention-seeking; like Wearside Jack, whose identity we now know, this man was revelling in the fact that he had stirred such huge number of police officers into action and caused emotional mayhem in the streets of Liverpool. 'Getting off' on that was so pleasant for him that other letters followed.

We can only feel glad that David Kirby was in his grave and missed this further torture.

CHAPTER 23

Women Campaigners in Walton Gaol

1909

Forcible feeding was threatened and Mrs Martin therefore barricaded her cell . . .

In August 1892, a woman prisoner at Walton Gaol was brought to appear before the committee of prison visitors. She had tried to wreck what she could in her cell and assaulted the matron. Her punishment for this misdemeanour was to be shackled for four days, with her hands tied behind her back. The Governor had directed the irons to be put on for a period without a limit, and that was his mistake. He was in the wrong. The case highlights the long history of brutal repression of women prisoners there.

Sidelights on history such as this make us wonder who committed the crimes in days long gone. Another seventeen years after this incident, and again in Walton, there were events which make us ask the question again. This was what the Women's Social and Political Union was to call 'Atrocities in an English Prison' in their newsletter. The writers

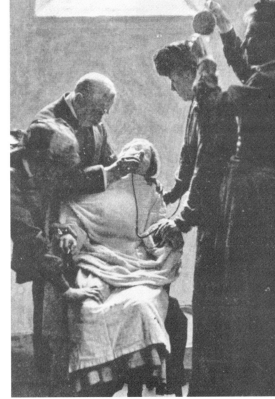

Force-feeding a suffragette. Author's collection

claimed that 'Two English women have been assaulted, knocked down, gagged, fed by force, kept for consecutive days and nights in irons.' The article was about Selina Martin and Leslie Hall who had been remanded in Walton for a week, bail being refused.

But the Suffragettes were to provide an even more sensational story in Liverpool, as a member of the top English aristocracy, Lady Constance Lytton, came up with a plan to be arrested and taken to Walton to experience and write about the kind of treatment that was being given to her fellow protesters for women's rights. Her father had been Viceroy of India, and her mother was at one time lady-in-waiting to Queen Victoria. Now here was Constance, a militant for the feminist cause, and she took on the identity of 'Jane Warton' when arrested in Liverpool. It was, from one point of view, an undercover job, an investigation, with herself as the subject of the 'atrocities' claimed.

Liverpool had not experienced a great deal of militancy over the period of activist campaigns; there would be only ten incidents in the city at one of the most energetic periods of unrest: 1913–14. Although Edith Rigby, a secretary of a branch of the WSPU, did place a pipe bomb at the Liverpool Exchange Building in 1913. The bomb actually exploded. It didn't do the general debate any good at all that Rigby's husband approved of what she was doing. Such events helped to cause more division and mistrust, but on the positive side it made the men with more entrenched conservative view sit up and take notice.

Real militancy in the campaign had started in October 1905, when Annie Kenney and Christabel Pankhurst heckled the MP Sir Edward Grey. They went to prison for a week, after refusing to pay a fine. From then onwards, the WSPU would have a militant 'wing.' Women in the regions were asked to participate more actively in local campaigns. Deputations to the House of Commons followed, and after 1909 the government began the 'force feeding' of women who were being held in Holloway. Then hundreds of women in all areas, were held and force-fed.

'Jane Warton' was born. There is a photograph of her, showing a tallish, thin women wearing a long black coat (with badges on the collar) and a large-brimmed hat to put a dark shade over face. It would have been hard to see the famous Lady Lytton under all that. Lytton went to Walton Gaol where there was a crowd, and with the intention of being arrested, she committed her 'crime', as she describes it in her memoirs: 'I took to running and urging on the crowd . . . I began discharging my stones, not throwing them but limply dropping them over the hedge into the governor's garden. Two policemen then held me fast by the arms and

VOTES FOR WOMEN

The Women's Social and Political Union

Head Office: 4, CLEMENTS INN, STRAND, W.C.

Telegraphic Address: "Wospolu, London."

Founder and Hon. Secretary—Mrs. PANKHURST.
Joint Hon. Secretary—Mrs. TUKE.
Publishing Office—THE WOMAN'S PRESS.
Bankers—Messrs. BARCLAY & CO., Fleet Street, E.C.

Hon. Treasurer—Mrs. PETHICK LAWRENCE.
Organising Secretary—Miss CHRISTABEL PANKHURST, LL.B.
Newspaper—VOTES FOR WOMEN.
Colours—PURPLE, WHITE, & GREEN.

Atrocities in an English Prison.

Two Englishwomen, unconvicted prisoners on remand in an English prison (Walton Gaol, Liverpool) have been assaulted, knocked down, gagged, fed by force, kept for consecutive days and nights in irons. One of them has been **frog-marched**. Frog-marched! What does that mean? Read the story.

The Facts.

On December 20th Miss Selina Martin and Miss Leslie Hall were arrested in Liverpool, and were remanded for one week, bail being refused.

Accordingly, while still unconvicted prisoners, they were sent to Walton Gaol, Liverpool. There, contrary to regulations, intercourse with their friends was denied to them. As unconvicted prisoners they refused to submit to the prison discipline or to take the prison food. Forcible feeding was threatened and Miss Martin therefore barricaded her cell. The officials, however, effected an entrance, fell upon her and handcuffed her, dragged her to a punishment cell and flung her on the floor, with her hands tightly fastened together behind her back.

Statement on prison atrocities. Author's collection

marched me off to the police station.' Lytton explained the reason for going to Liverpool: 'I was sent . . . to join in working an anti-government campaign during a general election in 1910. Just before I went, there came the news of the barbarous ill treatment of Miss Selina Martin and Miss Leslie Hall . . . I heard too of another prisoner in Liverpool, Miss Bertha Brewster who had been re-arrested after her release from prison, which she had done as a protest at being fed by force.'

The conditions in the gaol were harsh. She upset the authorities in lots of small ways, as in her attempt to combat the intense cold by wearing her skirt fastened around her neck. She wanted to speak to the governor when he made his first visit, but his windows had been broken in the protest outside, and he was in a bad mood. At least she had a gas-jet for some degree of light in that pokey, dark place, with its tiny high window.

Warton/Lytton refused food for four days when inside the prison. This meant that she would have to be force-fed, and her memoirs provide an account of what that was like: a gag was placed between her teeth, 'then he put a tube down her throat 'which seemed to me much too wide and was about four feet in length.' This is what happened next:

Then the food was poured in quickly; it made me sick a few seconds after it was down and the action of the sickness made my body and legs double up, but the wardresses instantly pressed back my head and the doctor leant on my knees. The horror of it was more than I

'A Troubled Dream of the Future', *Punch*, 1884. Author's collection

can describe. I was sick over the doctor and wardresses, and it seemed a long time before they took the tube out . . .'

This was so horrendous that reports about attempts at resistance make painful reading: 'Force feeding was threatened so Mrs Martin barricaded her cell' is the kind of sentence often encountered in reading these records. As for Jane Warton, she was 'found out' and attitudes changed, and so there was a furore. The doctor, knowing who she really was, said: 'You are absolutely not fit for this kind of thing. How could your Union send a woman like you to do a thing of this kind?' What better evidence could the militants have than this? The implication was that it was quite acceptable to force feed and manacle working class women, considered to be 'more robust'.

This issue and the general consequences of the Jane Warton case, led to energetic leaders and letters in *The Times*. On February 10 1910, the Home Secretary, Edward Troup, was forced to make a statement to the press. He wrote: 'I am directed

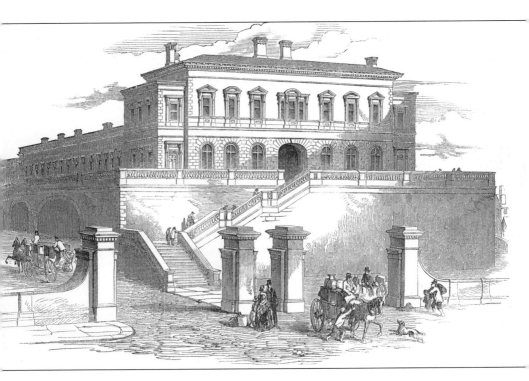

The Exchange Station as it was in 1850 - later a target of militants. *Illustrated London News*/Author's collection

by the Secretary of State to say that the statement that Lady Constance Lytton was released from Liverpool prison only when her identity was discovered was untrue. The release of "Jane Warton" was recommended by the medical officer . . . upon purely medical grounds.'

The facts are that Lytton was force fed eight times. She had been entered in the prison books as having refused medical examination, so how could the medical officer's assessment have been made? The case had highlighted more than the different treatment given to militants of different classes. It also brought to public attention the inhuman treatment of female prisoners that had been going on for decades, and in Liverpool some of the worst examples of this are on record. It was not illegal. The prison authorities were within the law, but that is a matter for debate as to the justness of such punishments as shackling for many days at a time.

As for Constance Lytton, she died in 1923, after being handicapped by paralysis eleven years before. Her last days in Walton included an interview with the governor and the doctor: she said that they were 'courteous' on that occasion. Her courage was incredible, and her time in Walton not only highlighted some of the inhumane treatment that had been part of the prison system for years, but also the sanctioned attitudes and treatment given out to women with startling callousness. Even the notorious death of Emily Davidson under the King's horse in the 1915 Derby had seemingly not changed some of these attitudes to female suffrage.

CHAPTER 24

The Wife-Killer Docker

1910

. . . he kicked her, picked her up and carried her out . . .

There are some ruthless killers in the annals of murder who have a strange element of dark humour in their personality. Sometimes this is a playful black humour of sheer resignation to fate; sometimes it comes from a relish in being perverse. The docker Henry Thompson was such a man. In 1910 he was fifty-four and lived with his wife and a woman lodger in York Street. On the morning of 31 July, the lodger said that Mary Thompson walked into her room and asked to be hidden from her husband.

There was something seriously wrong. Henry came in and saw his wife ducked down behind a bed. He took hold of her and pushed her out. The lodger must have been horrified, as the man then kicked his wife brutally. He kicked her, picked her up and carried her out.

Then the lodger heard various noises, scuffles and cries right through the following night. When things came to a head, she heard a muffled plea of 'Harry, don't choke me!' from the couple's bedroom and then, ominously, she heard the sound of something being dragged on the floor. The next day all was quiet, and the docker explained Mary's absence from the downstairs rooms by saying that it was her birthday and she was having a lie-in.

What happened next is like a scene from a horror film: the lodger was so worried that she crept into the bedroom late that following night, intending to check that Mary was all right. Thompson was sound asleep, so the woman stealthily moved close to Mary's legs, felt her flesh, and knew that the poor woman was stone cold. Was she dead? It seemed highly likely. Even more unlikely, but true, she went to fetch another woman from next door. The scene is more intensely frightening: two women now creeping into the room, to check for a corpse, while the killer sleeps on in bed. They were then sure that Mary was dead. The neighbour pulled back the bedclothes to look at the body.

The Canning Half-Tide Dock. The author

When this was reported and questions began to be asked, Thompson's eccentric and emotionless side came out. 'The bloody thing was lying like a stuffed dummy in the bed beside me', he said. His excuse that he thought she had had a fit after being very drunk the day before but he had no defence as the lodger had seen him behave in a terrifyingly violent way to the victim. The man appears to have had a death-wish, and was emotionally on the edge of reason from that point on. When in prison after a death-sentence he said to the doctor that he could have taken his own life at any point in that weekend when his wife lay dead in their home. More of his whimsical, deranged state came out when he told warders: 'I'll come back to this prison as a bird, as I am a Buddhist, to have a good look at you all . . .'

Thompson had even caused a fuss in court. When the clerk at Liverpool Assizes asked him if he had anything to say before sentence was passed he said: 'No let 'em get on with it. I don't care. I never was frightened of death.' Then he actually interrupted the judge as he put on the black cap and began to deliver the sentence. 'Yes my Lord . . .' he said, 'I'm not guilty.'

The bizarre behaviour continued to the very end in the death cell. He even clambered onto a chair in the execution suite, then jumped to the floor and said: 'I expect it will soon be over . . . It will only be summat like this.' The officers present were, of course, nonplussed by this behaviour. Most of their clients were pensive and subdued, concerned more with prayer or distractions than doing such a black role-play of their own death.

John Ellis, the hangman, wrote about Thompson in his auto-biography, saying that Thompson 'Walked to the scaffold the next morning with an air of utter unconcern, and I can honestly say I never hanged a cooler man in my life.' At one point, Ellis peeped into the man's condemned cell and was seen. Thompson knew that the notorious Dr Crippen was to be hanged the next day (by Ellis) and said: 'I'll be senior to him at the other shop!'

There was heavy irony and not a little black humour in Ellis's summing-up on this strange client of his: 'I suppose I ought to be grateful to him for his great consideration for me and my profession.'

CHAPTER 25

Death in the Church of Humanity

1913

Miss Crompton was lying dead with a bullet wound through her head . . .

William Macdonald, just twenty years old, was a carpenter who had several intellectual interests, among them 'Marxism and Positivism', the powerful creed of a sub-culture who met in Upper Parliament Street at their base called, grandly, the Church of Humanity. The young man therefore had strong social and political opinions, but he was looking for a cause on his own doorstep in Liverpool, and he found it in this splinter-group church. He was a man of great passion and profoundly extreme allegiances and affections.

The Positivists were led by Sidney Style, a local solicitor. They met weekly at 69 Hope Street, and it was at these gatherings that Macdonald met an older woman, the daughter of the founder of the group, Mary Crompton. She was forty-two. Macdonald did not tell her of his affection for her, and so we have the beginning of a strangely violent and ragingly sadistic sequence of events. Much of the problem was made worse by some of the odd rituals and conventions of the Church of Humanity.

Mary's father was Albert Crompton and a granddaughter of a Justice of the Peace, Sir Charles Crompton, who had died in 1865. When a young man called Paul Gaze, a church member, was orphaned when young, one of the rules of the Church came into play: a member had to be found who would act *in loco parentis*, as mentor and parent. Mary became this parent to Gaze. She obviously developed a close friendship with him and was often in his company, and when he went to work in Africa, she still kept in touch and was always his guiding hand in religious matters.

But this bond of friendship began to rankle with young Macdonald, who was loving Mary from a distance and allowing his feelings to implode in him, to divert and create all kinds of unhealthy emotions. It seems strange that, even when Gaze came home from Africa with a wife, Macdonald was still jealous. It is also clear that Macdonald was far from a loyal and unthinking member of the brotherhood. This seems quite understandable when we consider his Marxism. Members often considered him to be antagonistic and had problems in absorbing their beliefs.

The crisis in Macdonald's unbalanced life came nearer when Gaze and his wife, after coming to Liverpool, followed the Church's ruling that after a civil ceremony, a young married couple had to observe a probationary period of three months of celibacy. Gaze was living in lodgings and his new wife was staying with Mary Crompton until the three months were up. The young wife knew no English, she was Portuguese, and also spoke French. Again, it is the case that Mary was a good guide and mentor to the young woman in this strange foreign culture.

As this three-month period was coming to an end, things came to a head in the odd and dangerous mind of Macdonald. On 7 October 1913 he called at the house of the man who had first brought him into the fold at the Church of Humanity – Richard Price Roberts. Something had shifted all reason from Macdonald's mind and he went there with an intention to kill the man. He failed, in spite of one of the two fired bullets going into Roberts' head, and into his nose. Grove Street was the next stop, where he could find Gaze, and this time he shot the man dead in the hall.

At 81 Bedford Street South, the killer's spree continued, and this time it was Mary who was the victim. He shot her in the head and death was quick. The natural outcome of all this was turning the gun on himself, and he did so. It took him three hours to die. When they found Mary Crompton she was lying dead with a bullet-wound through her head.

At the inquest on 9 October, Mr Inglis had to hear Miss Huckwell say that she had identified the body of her friend Mary. The result was going to be obvious: wilful murder and suicide, but it was adjourned for a few days for further information to be gathered. It would surely be too complicated to look into exactly what it was that appealed to young people in this particular group of worshippers. Aldous Huxley, perhaps unfairly, said that the Positivist Church was 'Catholicism without Christianity.' All that can be said is that no-one can legislate for the new recruit to any religious sect: how to accommodate an individual who may have complex and most unhealthy reasons for seeking out the companionship in worship and togetherness such as the Church offered Macdonald.

Who could possibly have known that the young and bookish man who enjoyed critical debate would one day stop speculating with his mind and use a gun to come to some conclusions?

CHAPTER 26

The Body in a Sack

1913

Ball was an 'unlucky' murderer

Christina Bradfield, forty years old and manageress of a tarpaulin company on Old Hall Street, went missing from her lodgings. Her landlady, after a day had elapsed with no sign of her lodger, went to ask around the office and the warehouse. She was told that Christina had last been seen at 6.40 at the office, with two employees, George Ball and Samuel Eltoft. These two were questioned, and suspicions were aroused by the owner of the business, Mr Bradfield, when Ball told him that the firm's keys had been entrusted to him by Christina. Not only was this highly unlikely – there was something else. Ball had scratches on his face, as if he had been involved in a struggle.

The two men were only packers at the company, they were not in any managerial position, and in fact Eltoft had only worked there for a year. Fate was against George Ball, though. He was, in the words of Robert Jackson, the biographer of Lord Hewart who led the prosecution, 'an unlucky murderer.' This was because, on the day of the killing, a seaman called Walter Eaves stopped by the shop and as it was a windy day, a blind crashed down and ruined his new hat. When George Ball came outside to tend to the blind, Eaves insisted that he should be compensated for the hat. Eaves was given two shillings, but he was still around the area a little later and he saw Ball and Eltoft pushing a barrow with a heap of tarpaulin on it. They were really struggling, so it was something the seaman noticed and remembered later.

Later on, at a lock gate on the Leeds and Liverpool canal, a certain Francis Robinson saw a sack jamming the gate and when he dragged this free, he saw that there were two human feet sticking out. This was the body of Christina Bradfield. There was an umbrella with the initials CCB on it and also there was a necklace which helped to confirm her identity. She had been beaten to death. Ball had attacked her with a marline spike and stolen the takings. The body had been sewn into the sack.

Lord Hewart. Author's collection

There was a hunt for the two packers. Eltoft was found at his
lodgings but Ball had flown the nest and the chase for him would
take some time. At this time, there were picture palaces and news-
reels, images of wanted men could be circulated and shown to the
local population very quickly and effectively. All main newspapers
also had a description of him. But he was clever, and he realised
the importance of changing his appearance. Ball wore glasses and
what had once been distinctively thick eyebrows were snipped
back to thin strips; he even shaded a lens of the glasses pink. Only
someone who knew him well would have picked him out on the
Liverpool streets – and he did boldly stay in Liverpool in this new
identity.

Ten days after the search began, his luck ran out, as someone who knew him did indeed see him. He was seen in a pub on St James Street and reported to the police. Of course, Eaves was a crucial witness, as was the typist who last saw Ball and Eltoft with the victim. But he had no chance when the dead woman's watch was found on him, and also other witnesses came forward.

The trial took place from on 2 – 5 February before Mister Justice Atkin. Gordon Hewart for the prosecution was troubled by the case, as his biographer explains: 'What surprised his friends at the time of the Ball trial was that Hewart should have been so affected by the public hysteria over the case that he allowed himself to doubt the clear evidence he produced as a prosecutor . . .' The story with regard to young Eltoft was that Ball had sent him out to get a handcart for the rubbish, and that when Eltoft came back he saw the murder scene and was stunned, saying: 'It looks rather black against us.' Ball made it clear that the man would have to be involved, as he would be sure to be blamed – just for being there.

Ball could only muster an incredible story about a tough stranger arriving while Ball and Eltoft were upstairs, the stranger supposedly standing with a marline spike and demanding cash. The fact was, as Ball's landlord had stated, on that night Ball had returned to his digs two hours later than usual – and with cuts to his face. Hewart's prosecution case was not going to be difficult, as long as the plausible inventions of this wily villain did not win over the jury.

It backed up the general picture of Eltoft that when he was arrested, he expressed no knowledge as to why they would come for him. Ball was the one who had embellished the unlikely tale of the stranger, and this was a desperate ploy in the face of so much evidence stacked against him. Hewart knew that the main motive – robbery – was easily linked to Ball since he was very hard-up and had even borrowed three pence a day from his landlady to pay for his tram rides to work.

But Ball kept on fabricating not only the story of the murderous stranger, but also creating a view of himself and Miss Bradfield which seemed to suggest immense respect and co-operation at work. At first Ball's account of the supposed killer was quite convincing. He lied so well that the jury were ready to accept the tale, but Hewart pushed him so that, when cornered, he began to say that there was a second man, backing up the killer with the marline spike. It then became clear that Ball would start inventing stories again. He even tried to convince everyone in the court that he had gone into disguise to save Eltoft, saying 'they could not do anything with Eltoft until they got me . . .' Hewart, in his final speech, addressed the jury with these words: 'If his story is not true it is clear that you are dealing with no mere artificer in crime, but with a master of the craft. The story he has told you makes excessive demands on your credulity.'

Ball was sentenced to death and Eltoft given four years penal servitude for concealment. But there is an ironical coda to Eltoft's story. A detective went to Eltoft's parents' house just to check out the young man's room again. Something had led him to take a second look. Sure enough, as he unscrewed a bedstead brass knob, he found inside two and a half sovereigns. This information could have radically altered Eltoft's sentence. What it did do was forestall his appeal, as that detail, given at an appeal, would have cancelled the whole business and coloured everyone's views of the man who helped in the murder. In some accounts, even today, there are distortions in print about Eltoft, some thinking that he was 'feeble-minded.' The fact is that Hewart worried and lost sleep over the issue of the man's innocence. He had most likely been threatened and coerced into assisting in the terrible slaying of his employer, but there were lingering doubts.

When the time for the execution drew hear, in Walton Gaol, Ball confessed everything to Dr Chavasse, Bishop of Liverpool. He was yet another client for the Rochdale hangman, John Ellis.

CHAPTER 27

Murder of a Nurse

1919

Two gun shots were fired and a woman was heard screaming . . .

Some kinds of love can be like handling explosives. What some call love can be no more than manic possession. One man in the criminal history of Liverpool had huge problems with his definition of love, and in the end, he had to do what Shakespeare made his tragic hero Othello do, kill his one beloved. Like Othello, this man was a victim of the 'green-eyed goddess'.

Joseph Hutty, when he came to the Northern Hospital in 1918 with severe injuries to his legs, was definitely a hero; he had shell-shock as well, and he had performed the amazing feat of carrying another soldier out of the battle zone to safety, shells bursting around him as he staggered clear. He was just twenty-three when he came into the care of nurse Alice Kate Jones (known as Kitty), a woman of his age who had come to Liverpool from Newhey, Lancashire, to complete her professional training. She was strikingly attractive and the patients all thought her to be a wonderful nurse.

Hutty was from Detriot, but he had enrolled with a Canadian regiment. Some of the most daring and dashing acts of rash heroism had been done by Canadians, including one officer who actually caught grenades and threw them back at the enemy. Hutty was in this class, a man in need of something grand and passionate in his life. In this case it was the familiar scenario of the wounded soldier being smitten with affection for his nurse. They developed a close relationship as his health improved. They met as Joseph was getting in some walking practice, his crutches scraping the floor of the long hall between wards. The friendship did not end when he was taken to another hospital and they corresponded. The turning point came when Joseph went to visit Kate at her family home, and there he asked her father for her hand in marriage. The response to that was indicative of the course of his true love never running smoothly – Kitty's father told him that he approved of the match, but that he wanted his daughter to qualify first. That meant waiting, and Hutty was not good at waiting for anything.

A campaign of increasingly fulsome, emotional and insistent letters began to pour from Hutty's hospital bed when he went back across the Atlantic to Toronto. The general tone of these is about possession. It was a classic example of the lover who moves too quickly and intensely towards that kind of one-sided relationship that imparts a degree of fear. He wrote such things as: 'In one letter you cannot come over too soon and the next you don't give a damn how long it is before you come to me. You are a puzzle . . .'

For some time the affection was mutual, though, and Kitty wrote about wanting to see him and ruffle his hair. When their emotions were equally matched and there was a rapport between them she wrote and used the word marriage. But she stopped writing early in March 1919. Her silence was the lull before the inevitable 'Dear John' letter which was such a cliché for the thousands of soldiers who had had liaisons in the climate of world war. Kate wrote:

> *I have come to a great decision, one which hurts me very much and also one which is quite final. I shall never marry you. Please don't ask me the reason why. I can tell you this: there is certainly no-one else . . .*

It was certainly not a sugar-coated message, but in this brutal honesty, it was clear that the young woman had good intentions, trying to follow the 'cruel to be kind' rule in such matters. For Hutty it was only the beginning of his long losing battle against keeping on a struggle to have her, to win her back, and by any means. In July he was back in Liverpool, and ready to begin a season of sheer nuisance-making obsession. He clearly had the make-up of a dangerous stalker. He wrote to her, even threatening suicide, and he pestered people who knew her. Kitty must have sensed that there was still a deep menace in this man, even though he wrote to say: 'If my mother writes to you, or your people, let her know what happened to me. I will say goodbyes now, Joe.'

Kitty felt that this was not goodbye at all, and she was so nervous when she planned to come back to Liverpool after some 'time out' of this dreadful harassment back home in Newhey, that she arranged for a friend to meet her train. This was Frank Schoo, a man she had spent some time with. He was chief officer of the USS *Andalucia* docked in the city. On 24 July she did arrive at the Exchange Station and there was Schoo. But Hutty was a man

The Exchange Station today.
The author

full of the wit and cunning of a deranged and obsessive mind. He was there, like a shadow, waiting for the moment to pounce, by the hospital steps, as if he had an instinct about where the couple would walk when they came from the station. He just said, 'Nurse Jones?' As Kitty turned, four shots were fired into her and she fell. Hutty had been drinking with a friend, McMahon, who said that the two of them had been loitering around the hospital, waiting for Kitty to come onto her night shift. Then Hutty had taken off on his evil, murderous mission.

Another witness just said: 'Four gunshots were fired and a woman was heard screaming.'

Hutty ran off, but he confessed to the nearest constable. Maybe his death-wish was genuine at the time. DS Case checked out the story and he knew that he had a homicide solved in a very short time indeed. His pistol had been thrown down but it was recovered and it related well to the situation of the killing.

In the phase of Hutty's life in and leading up to the trial, his personality became more complex and whimsical than ever, even to the point of his blaming a rash on his face on Kitty, as a source of venereal disease. Medical statements soon dismissed this. The telling moment in the whole trial was when a barrister asked Hutty if he was 'in love with this woman?' Hutty began to sob and hid his face from view. But he had thought enough to explain why he was carrying a pistol that night, saying it was for protection against a rowdy gang of Americans in town.

This was certainly a planned and wilful murder; the only potential defence was going to be if the accused's shellshock was a meaningful factor in the crime. There had been a number of cases of shell-shock soldiers who had murdered wives and girlfriends in the years just after the Great War, but all their circumstances were different. Reprieve was never a certainty in these instances. But the basic fact expressed by the judge in court was that any flimsy defence of his crime being an 'uncontrollable impulse' (the defence lawyers used this phrase which had been spoken by a doctor in the case).

The judge simply said that all crime was enacted under some kind of 'uncontrollable impulse' so why should this be any different? He even considered the case to be a perfectly everyday case of a jealous man wanting that only power left to him – to kill, so that another could not have what he himself could not have. Hutty was sentenced to hang. But the tale does not end there. Maybe due to his war record and perhaps with some reference to the neurasthenia he had suffered for so long, a petition for reprieve was gathered and it had the desired effect. There were over three thousand signatures, and these included that of the Lord Mayor of Liverpool.

Hutty's sentence became life imprisonment, and so he was given plenty of time to feel the torment of having killed the one person he professed to love.

CHAPTER 28

Riots, Strikes and Violence

1911–1919

On the corner of Scotland Road, ominous gangs were gathering . . .

There can be few English cities which have experienced the sheer variety of public disorder that Liverpool suffered in the Edwardian period. Not only was there industrial strife, there was also a serious confrontation between the Catholic and Protestant factions, as well as a violent response to the *Lusitania* sinking. All too often there were troops on the streets and extra police brought in to deal with the scale of this rioting and brawling. As usual in these affairs, the victims

A reminder of the Irish cultural base of the city - in Matthew Street, near the Cavern. The author

were either people caught up in the roughest part of the trouble, or officers of the law trying to do their duty.

In 1909, the street violence was all about religion. In a city in which such massive Irish immigration has taken place, then logically the political and religious affiliations come with them. Street marches and public worship may easily ignite trouble. In most Lancashire towns in the Victorian and Edwardian period, marches and floats, with music, were a common sight in the streets. Sometimes it led to very nasty assaults. Liverpool had its Orangemen and its Catholic societies. Any show of public allegiance or brotherhood would have to be tactfully handled by the authorities.

The heart of the trouble was when the congregation of the Church of the Holy Cross planned to celebrate the sixtieth anniversary of the founding of their Mission by holding an event in the Great Crosshall Street area. A request was put in to the

Troops arrive to crush the riots. Laura Carter

Health Committee for a procession to be held, with garlands en route, and for an altar to be placed by the fountain at the junction of Marylebone and Standish Street. A simple failure in communication of knowledge was to lead to public disorder. The police chief knew nothing about the permission given to the Catholic group to have an altar by the fountain. That permission had been given by the Health Committee. By the time that a Mr Boulter wrote to the Chief Constable (on 30 April) the event was very soon to happen, and when the Constable talked with the Committee representative, they misunderstood the nature of the altar.

The result was that most thought that there would be no Catholic ceremonial; then things were made worse by another element – that of George Wise. It so happened that Wise had control of a Protestant Crusade at the time. The man seems to have had some irrational political perspective on the Catholic Church, and he was to play a part in the disastrous events which happened when the altar was seen in the street.

The Chief Constable was away from town on 20 June when Pastor Wise, the Orangemen and the Catholic group were in the streets and not at all happy. Mr Lane, Assistant Constable, did his best to avoid problems, but despite an increase in the police presence from 250 to 700 men, the worst fears were realised. A crowd gathered in Juvenal Street East and the police clashed with the mob. Then, in Prince Edwin Street, there was a disgraceful scene of anarchy as mounted police charged the unruly crowd. This was in the afternoon. The riot went on until late in the night. Around fifty people were arrested, and such was the turbulence of the crowd and the fighting that Lane had a force of a thousand men at his command, many of them escorting some marchers to safety. But things were nasty. One officer was stabbed in the back and another had a broken jaw.

Through many nights in June there were attacks and skirmishes on various quarters of the city. Mr Wise was not happy about what he considered to be undue violence by police and by Catholics against the Orangemen. Such was the feeling whipped up by Wise in court, where he was given a fine and was bound over to keep the peace that there was a clamour for a public inquiry into the police actions at the worst stage of the rioting. But when questions were asked, it became obvious that the police had to take extreme measures when they were attacked in extreme ways. In Beresford Street, it was found, gangs of men had iron bars and a brick wall was pulled down to provide missiles for attack on officers.

In 1911 the trouble was all about strikes and sympathetic industrial action. On 14 June Liverpool seamen went on strike, for higher wages. Other trades followed in support. The centre of the action was a massive throng towards support of the National Union of Dock Labourers. By August the railwaymen had joined in. Things came to a head, as they usually do in these matters, when a huge crowd gathered to hear speeches at St George's Plateau. There were 80,000 people in the streets when panic set in and the worst thing imaginable happened: the police charged the crowd with batons. It would not be too strong a comment to say that there was anarchy in Liverpool for a week. The military were brought in, and a warship. HMS *Antrim*, was placed ready in the Mersey. Survival was tough for many and desperate days led to desperate actions. The height of the disorder was when shots rang out and two men were injured in a prison van as it took men to Walton prison.

At least all this mayhem led to something positive – widespread enrolment in the unions. The syndicalist James Larkin (Liverpool-born) had a huge popular following in Liverpool and in Dublin; the strikes, along with his tough attitudes for the workers, led to an increase of almost a million people in union membership between 1910 and 1911. The punch-ups and panic in the streets were not entirely useless.

In May 1915, the liner *Lusitania* was sunk by a German submarine, after sailing out of Liverpool. The outrage after this was savage and irrational. Anything German in the land was hated and shopkeepers with German names were to find their property smashed or to find that they would be attacked if they walked out in the street. *The Weekly Dispatch* wrote, 'How many Germans are living in this country and are not in gaol?'

In Liverpool, as Pat O'Mara has written, 'On the corner of Scotland Road ominous gangs were gathering . . .' The reason was that many of the dead were from that area. O'Mara recalled hearing the cries and moans of people around the Scotland Road area who had lost loved ones in the disaster. In Bostock Street, almost every home had blinds or curtains drawn close as a sign of a death. The men who had died were mostly Irish coal-trimmers, sailors and firemen from the ship. Mr Taylor, who had been a steward on Cunard ships, recalled that on the day after the disaster there were photographs of bodies in the basement of a building in Rumford Street. He noted, 'One I particularly remember of a young woman lying with her baby in her arms, but many of the photographs were too horrible for words.'

The gangs were out to beat up anyone who might be considered to be German, so that included anyone with an un-English and vaguely European name. Properties with German links were naturally prime targets. As the gangs were out, dozens of shops were attacked and police in the city made sixty-seven arrests. Later, Liverpool Corporation was to receive over 500 compensation claims from residents.

Arguably the worst riots took place in 1919 when again there were armed officers in the streets. In the first days of August of that year there was looting of shops when the poor families of the Scotland Road area came out to exploit the situation. *The Times* reported that the poor people took pianos and 'thumped them in a frenzied endeavour to demonstrate their defiance of law and order.' There were armoured cars in the streets, and from one of these, a magistrate read the Riot Act. There were no less than 370 arrests.

Causes of the trouble were not hard to find. After the Great War, massive numbers of demobbed soldiers came home to unemployment and deprivation. They had to find a way to express their discontent and disillusion and street violence was the simplest and most effective way to do this. Such rioting had happened across the land – not just in Liverpool. One woman, Nellie Wallace, told writer Steve Humphries that she was working as a barrow girl when she was ten in Liverpool and that 'Every shop was smashed in . . . We had pieces of lovely bacon in the streets and the people was hungry. . . . You'd see the things all scattered around and everyone run with the stuff in their hands . . .' But the retribution was to come. The army and police were ruthless in their search for culprits. Nellie said: 'They searched everything. Even dragged your beds out to see if there was any loot. My mother had this big long-john full of bacon and she had it on the fire.'

CHAPTER 29

The McKenzie Murder

1921

The man saw a woman's legs.. there was a body under the bed

This is a Liverpool story, but it involves a detective from the city trailing a man across the North Sea to Antwerp and then having to hold the man until there was extradition; the killer he was after may well have slipped away. It is a tense and exciting tale, though at its heart is a morbid and everyday killing.

In May 1921 Mary Pannell advertised a room to let in her large Victorian property at 14 Brownlow Street. It was common practice then to let out rooms, and Liverpool was a busy commercial city with thousands of travelling men coming and going on commercial transactions. She soon had a response and a man with a foreign accent, wearing a bushy moustache, came to call. He was middle-aged and, strangely, brought no luggage with him. But he was quiet, well-mannered and smartly turned-out. He gave his name as John Brown and explained that he was in the sales business, concerned with textiles. He accepted the rent of ten shillings a week and was given a key.

Brown came and went at all hours and was usually out for most of the evenings. Sometimes he was away from the flat for several days and he explained this by saying that his sister was a woman who needed him to nurse her, as she had nobody else. All this added to the generally good opinion formed of the quiet man of mystery at number fourteen. In July he turned up with a woman whom he announced as being the sister he had spoken of previously. She was a thick-set, middle-aged woman who talked of her heart problems. The story was that she had had to retire from any regular work due to the deteriorating state of her health. The couple were seen around the area by several people and so everything about them seemed normal. But on 16 July, when she went to do the housework in Brown's room, the door was locked, and was still locked five days later when she tried again. Had the man left without paying his rent? Miss Pannell naturally thought that

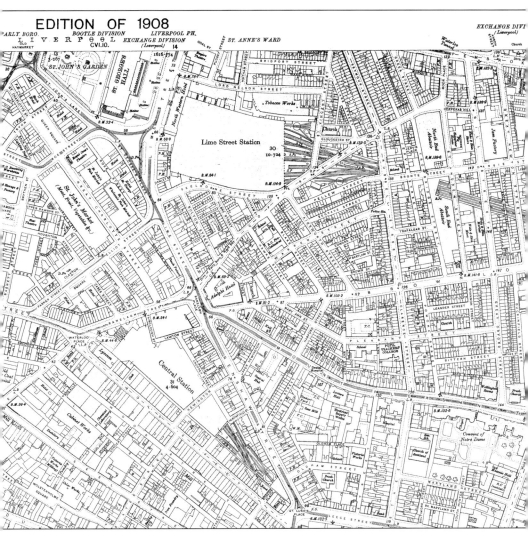

The area south of Lime Street Station in 1908. Ordnance Survey

because his rent was due on the day she went again to clean for him.

When a lodger called Grant was asked to go around and enter the room by the outside window, a shock was coming to the residents of 14 Brownlow Street. The man at the window saw a woman's legs on the floor – he felt certain that there was a body under the bed. The lodger, Grant, rammed the window open and it was then that he experienced a rank smell – from a body which had been there for some time. He wasted no time in calling for the police.

The first detective on the scene noted that the body was cut to pieces and that there was only one garment on the corpse – a chemise. She was lying in a pool of blood, and the most repulsive detail on the scene of horror was a little heap of flesh by the body. 'I thought it was rats' urine, as it dries like a little hill . . .' he said. But it turned out to be the genital organs, neatly taken out. Her throat had been cut. But there were several other cuts on the jaw, chin and neck. A forensic report of the time notes that 'The wounds were putrefying and were covered with mould . . . On the left side of the wound and upon the left thigh were some abrasions as if scraped by a sharp instrument.'

Miss Pannell identified the body as that of the person introduced to her as Brown's sister. It was a strong and vicious attack, but the wounds were mostly done after death, and with a clean instrument. The person the police were looking for was some kind of obsessed or perverted fetishist, it seemed. A clean instrument had been used to take out the genitals. It was a macabre business cleaning up the room. The mattress was soaked in blood and there were clothes littered around, mostly bloodied.

Some little objects found in some of the clothes provided some leads, though. One of the most interesting, bearing in mind Brown's foreign accent, was the name 'E. Braem' with a Liverpool address. There was also a false lead, to a seaman called Nicholson, but the turning-point in the first enquiries came when the identity of the dead woman was confirmed. She was Mary Sarah McKenzie Clarke, apparently not 'on the game', but a known heavy drinker, and objects found in her lodgings made it certain that she was living by doing thefts from motor vehicles. Then, from markings on collars in the room at Brownlow Street, details of another place used by Brown were found. This was at 40 Guelph Street. The man of mystery was indeed a puzzle for the law.

But the lead that led to Brown being traced was found, courtesy of the paperwork required by the Aliens Act of 1905. 'Brown' had had to fill in a form. This revealed that he was really Mr Braem of Courtrai in Belgium. He had given his date of birth, an Antwerp address and a note that he had served in the Belgian army as a lancer. Not only did the form lead to useful information; there was a central register of aliens in London. The Home Office then stated that Braem had a record. In Sheffield he had been arrested for living by false pretences. Then the police even had a photograph of him, held at the Criminal Records Office – he had served a short gaol sentence.

The chase was on in earnest now. A detective went to the Antwerp address and he was tracked down; in his possession were press cuttings about the Liverpool murder. Of course, on arrest, he told a story – that a man called Fisher from Manchester had done the murder. With the Belgian authorities insisting on a proper extradition order, DCS McCoy was desperate for his superiors in Liverpool to have a warrant and extradition papers from home. Finally these came, and were signed by the Prosecuting Solicitor back home.

Meanwhile, the hunt for the supposed 'Fisher' went on and at first there was no result, even after a methodical search for all people named Fisher in Manchester. Eventually, by sheer persistence, officers came across a sailor called Harry Fisher, and a thorough questioning made it clear that this man had indeed been a drinking acquaintance of Braem; but there it ended. There was no more to it. Braem had said that Fisher was Australian, and this sailor worked for a steamship company operating between Liverpool and Australia. It was soon obvious that Braem had fabricated a personality from the actual Harry Fisher, the genial drinker and talker. In fact, in Antwerp, Braem could not identify Fisher from a picture shown him in a sequence of images. Detective McCoy had earned his pay with all his hard work on the case.

After more testing at the scene of crime, and with Belgian officers present, it was found that any noise in the killing would not have been heard, as the next room was lived in by a man who was deaf and very ill. It was all over for Braem. It was in 1922 that he was finally sentenced, but he escaped the noose, despite the verdict of guilty of wilful murder. Medical circumstances saved his neck and he was given penal servitude for life.

CHAPTER 30

A Man Beset by Demons: Lock Ah Tam

1926

Where love had been, there was now merciless slaughter . . .

Some crimes in the murder casebooks read like fables; they resonate with that sense of fate and tragedy that marks some of the great literature of the world. Sometimes these tales concern men who have found wealth or celebrity and then fallen to ruin and failure. Others are about the rise and fall of power. But some are strongly human stories with possibilities for speculation about 'blame' and cause' when the happiness and fulfilment turn to disaster and pain. The story of Loch Ah Tam has this quality of a parable, a rise and a fall, and with a flaw in him that may have been a cause we can identify.

Tam was at first a desk clerk in a shipping office, having been born in Canton. In his early twenties he settled to work on land rather than at sea and he prospered. He had special gifts of charm, communication and efficiency and he did so well that by 1907 he had reached a very high status indeed – no less a person than the main man with the European union for Chinese stevedores, and also a major figure in the Chinese Republican Society, known properly as the Kock Man Tong. He acquired wealth and social status, settling in an old house in Birkenhead with his Welsh wife Catherine. They had three children: Lock Ling, Doris and Cecilia. He was more than a happy family man, however. Tam was a character in the city, a known 'good soul' who enjoyed talk, entertainment and caring for the poor who crossed his path. He was well-known for giving coins to poor children.

Our fable is fine so far: a portrait of a man with many reasons to be happy and content. He had a successful public life and a private family life that gave him immense pleasure. Then came the first sign that there might be a dark shadow over him and it led to an event that remains a debatable issue to this day when the story is told. He took control of a club which was intended as a

The gate at the entrance to China Town. The author

safe and cushioned environment for Chinese sailors coming to the city. This Chinese Progress Club involved Tam in the kind of responsibility that can lead to stress, and it couldn't have been more stressful than the night when a rowdy bunch of Russian sailors burst in looking for trouble. Tam stood up to them and, for his courage, he was given a heavy blow on the head with a billiard cue.

The nice Dr Jekyll faded from Tam's character and malevolent Mr Hyde began to invade his moods. The cordial, sociable man became temperamental and tetchy. The worst thing about him was that he was unpredictable. One time he responded to an innocent comment at a dinner party with a violent show of temper,

Upper Duke Street, where the Chinese Club was located. The author

smashing all the glasses on the table into the fireplace, then when the fury had passed, he receded into a torpor. To the family, it must have seemed as if a stranger had invaded their father.

The involvement of fate then became more cruel than ever: the arrival of financial problems hit Tam hard. He unwisely invested a huge sum of money, £10,000, into a shipping company which failed. In modern terms, he had lost perhaps a quarter of a million pounds.

Then came Christmas, 1925. Christmas had always been his favourite time of the year. He was used to playing the benevolent local philanthropist and he usually lavished time and money on people. But then, as his son returned home from a long spell in China, there was to be a Christmas so terrible that there was to be a horrendous scene of carnage in Tam's comfortable home. Where love had been there was now merciless slaughter and crazed shooting. When all the guests had gone, and everything had

The Chinese Community Centre today. The author

seemed quite normal with the genial host all night, there was a noise heard in the Tam bedroom. He was in a fury, and his son intervened, taking the women of the house to safety downstairs. We know that a worker in the house, Margaret, saw Tam with a gun, and also saw his demoniacal reflection in a mirror.

All the people in the house sensed something awful was about to happen. They cowered in fear as he prowled around the place. Young Lock tried to persuade his mother to creep out to the neighbours' house until this fit ended. But she stayed. When Margaret and the others were barricaded in the lounge, the terror really started. Tam slammed on the door and screamed at them. Lock and the neighbour, Mrs Chin, had come to the kitchen, trying to plan a way of resolving all this mayhem. When the others crept to them in that room, Lock took the opportunity to run out and look for a police officer.

The women were vulnerable, and the furious, crazed Tam now came at them, carrying a shotgun and a revolver. He shot, and Mrs Tam fell down dead; a second shot hit Cecilia with a mortal wound; then in the scullery he found his other daughter Doris, and she was mercilessly gunned down.

The 'fable' ends with a strange and chilling anti-climax, because Tam walked calmly to the phone and asked for officers to come for him. On the phone, he said simply: 'I have shot my wife and children. Please put me on to the Town Hall.' He was in a gaol cell before morning. When the officers came to take him, he stood there, calm, and smoking a cigarette.

This astonishing case naturally led to the professionals involved in Tam's defence looking back to that confrontation with the drunken sailors in the Chinese club. In fact, his defence counsel, Sir Edward Marshall Hall, went so far as to introduce the rare defence of automatism, and in a context of a claim of the condition being 'epileptic automatism.' Automatism is understood in law as a state of mind which takes away an individual's ability to be aware and do a voluntary action. A crime committed during a sleepwalking trance would be a typical example of this. When it comes to discussing this concept (and applying it) in a court of law, then the decisive factor is to sort out whether or not the state of the person at the time of the act involved anything that would make the crime self-induced. Lock Ah Tam's mental condition, Hall argued, was defective as a result of the attack by the Russian sailor in the club attack.

Unfortunately, the jury were not convinced. It took them only twelve minutes to reach a verdict: guilty. As the death sentence was given, Lock was very calm, in spite of his Chinese friends groaning in dismay in that atmospheric courtroom at the Chester Assizes. The prosecuting counsel, Sir Ellis Griffith, had had an easy task.

Lock was hanged in Liverpool on 23 March, 1926 by William Willis.

But there is plenty of evidence of what Lock achieved in his good phase. One Testimony comes from L K Loh, speaking in the Liverpool Shanghai Community Survey of 1926. He said:

Liverpool was the headquarters of the Blue Funnel Line. We stayed there waiting for the return ship to Shanghai. The boarding house was Next to the church in Upper Duke Street. The rooms were big – some rooms were Shared by five or six people. After we arrived at the boarding-house, the local Chinese gave us a warm welcome.

One feels that Lock Ah Tam was part of that.

CHAPTER 31

The Wallace Mystery

1931

Julia Wallace lay in a pool of her own blood, in her cosy room . . .

I f Liverpool can claim to be the setting for several infamous and problematic homicides, then first among these has to be the Wallace case. The year 1931 was notable for crime mysteries. There was the notorious 'Blazing Car' case in Northumberland, still unsolved, and also the Margaret Schofield case in Dewsbury (unsolved). But in sheer complexity, the death that has been called by many 'the perfect murder' is Liverpool's own, and presents the historian with a riddle: if William Wallace, gentle chess-playing insurance agent living in a quiet suburb, did indeed create an alibi and a hoax, then why did he make it all so difficult for himself? There were easier ways to create a ruse and a suspicious stranger.

The story began on 19 January 1931, when a phone call was made to the Central Chess Club in Liverpool by a man calling himself Qualtrough. He wanted to see Wallace urgently, on a business matter. Wallace was not yet at his

Wallace, the man from the 'Pru'.
Laura Carter

club, but he was due to arrive to play a match at seven o'clock. Wallace arrived at twenty-to-eight, and then he was told about the phone call. The club was at the City Café, and Wallace had not been doing too well of late, walking the streets for the Prudential. This call meant a potential customer, so he asked about the address given. Here lies the heart of the mystery: Qualtrough said he lived at Menlove Gardens East – an address that did not exist. Wallace asked several people about the address, and it was known that there was a street called Menlove Gardens North.

All this became important when Wallace's steps are traced the next day, when he went in search of the mystery man. He left his home in Wolverton Street and went to Smithdown Road; then he caught a number 4 tram at Lodge Lane. We know that he went to Menlove Gardens and started looking for 'East' in the area. He made a point of asking lots of people about the address. But by eight he had given up and went home. It was when he arrived home, just before nine, that he found the body of his wife. Julia Wallace lay in a pool of her own blood, in her cosy room.

The Wallaces were a quiet couple. Neighbours reported no

Menlove Avenue. Laura Carter

scenes of anger or disagreement. William was a bookish man. He read the works of Marcus Aurelius and based his behaviour and attitudes on that Roman's stoical philosophy. He was firm and controlled right through the coming investigation and trial, something that was surely against him. The image he gave was of a callous, unfeeling man, who should have shown extreme emotion after the violent killing of his wife in their own home. Wallace had been born in the Lake District in 1878. He had worked for a short while in India, and then in Ripon, before settling down to the life of a clerk in Liverpool, and married Julia in 1913.

The scene of crime was horrific. When Wallace came home, he could not open the front door, so he went around to the back. He managed to enter, walked upstairs, and found nothing unusual, but when he went down to the parlour and turned on the light, there was her body, lying face down on the rug. There was a pool of blood around her head and such was the force of a blow to her head that bone was visible. Wallace was accompanied by a friend, Jack Johnson, as he saw this, and Johnson went to bring a police officer. Meanwhile Wallace realised that his insurance takings had been stolen from a box in the kitchen. But it was puzzling that a jar of pound notes in the bedroom had not been taken, despite the fact that they were smudged with blood.

When PC Williams arrived, he and Wallace checked details, but then the forensic expert came, Professor MacFall. He discovered no less than ten more wound marks on the head. There was a mess in the house – evidence of an apparent frenzy. But MacFall noted that the gas-lights were out, so the rage and the supposed search for booty would have taken place in the dark. Also, there were no blood-marks in

Julia Wallace. Laura Carter

places where one would have expected them, such as on door-handles for instance.

Clearly, Wallace himself would have to be questioned intensively, as there were so many pointers to an alibi and so many oddities at the scene of the murder that did not seem to square with the supposed crazed murder and attack. D S Hubert Moore led the investigation. He had long experience, over thirty years of police work. At Dale Street police station, the interviews began. Attention was paid to the Qualtrough call, and to the witnesses who recalled talking to Wallace on his hopeless quest for Menlove Gardens East. It all appeared to be so fabricated, after all: a phone call at a point when there would be an alibi and yet enough time for Wallace to have made the call himself before arriving at the chess club; then all that asking for directions even to the point of making sure that conversations were memorable. It must have all seemed so purposeful to Moore as he faced this quiet, restrained and inscrutable man who controlled his emotions with perfection.

Amazingly, the Qualtrough phone call was traced. It was made from a box defined as Anfield 1627 – a box only four hundred yards from Wallace's house in Wolverton Street. But evidence at the scene was unavailable: there was no weapon, no prints and no items found even in the drains and sewers. It was noted, though, that a poker was missing. More important, what would be the motive? Julia had only £20 due from insurance on her life. Wallace had no need of that, he had money saved in his account. At the trial, people started looking for motives in the area of personality and relationship, even to noting Wallace's diary entries, such as one comment about Julia's 'aimless chatter.' But in context, he had written this after her death, saying that he missed her 'loving smiles and aimless chatter.'

The trial began on 22 April at St George's Hall. The judge was Mr Justice Wright; for the prosecution there was EG Hemmerde, and Roland Oliver for the defence. They were all brilliant lawyers in their way, but they were to find several anomalies and un-answered questions in this affair. Wallace's own statement included his own assertion that any hint of him having killed his wife was 'monstrous.' In gathering evidence for the defence, they had to concentrate on the timing of a milk delivery at the murder house. A certain Elsie Wright who was sure that the call at the house, at which Julia was alive, was close to a quarter to seven, not half past six. Little details such as this would count for a great deal in the case, as everything rested on the movements of Wallace around Liverpool that day.

Everything except the issue of the raincoat. Wallace's mackin-

An early monograph about the Wallace case.
Clifford Elmer Books

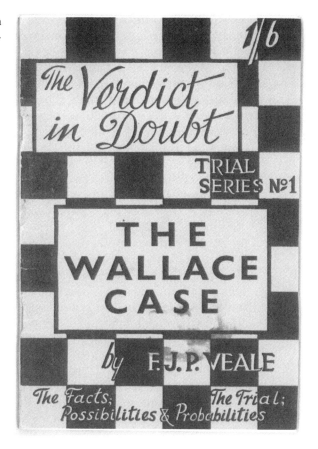

tosh was under Julia's body. Here, the limitations of forensics at the time were exposed, particularly in blood movements and splattering, the blood on this coat being either caused by the wounding, or in fact dripping there after death. There were also burn stains on the coat, so another question arose: did Wallace fail in an attempt to burn the material? Or equally sensible was the line of thought that it could have been burned in the attack, because Julia was close to the gas fire.

The questioning by the prosecution was aimed at locating all the strange and oddly convenient circumstances of the phone call, the attempt to find the address, and the arguably transparent and feeble creation of an alibi. It had also seemed unconvincing that an innocent man would have walked upstairs in his home before going through to the parlour; the implication being that he was fabricating a likely 'geography' of the movements of the supposed frenzied attacker. Equally, in the examination of Julia Wallace's nature and character, it had been made extremely unlikely that she would have a lover, so if the motive of the anonymous killer was related to a crime of passion, then where was the evidence for that? In the early afternoon of the fourth day of the trial, the jury retired to consider their verdict. Their decision was that Wallace was guilty of wilful murder. The judge stated that it was a 'murder unexampled in the annals of crime.'

After the death sentence was passed, Wallace still showed no response. *The Liverpool Post and Echo* reported that 'Wallace's bearing after the verdict was as calm and impassive as throughout the trial, and when asked if he had anything to say, he replied in a quiet tone: "I am not guilty. I don't want to say anything else."'

But that is not the end of the story. At the Court of Appeal on 19 May 1931, his case was reconsidered. This was after he was moved to Pentonville in April, and after prayers were said for him in Liverpool Cathedral. He played the violin and, as death was looming, his violin and his chess set had been brought to him. In Pentonville, though, he was housed in the death cell.

Hemmerde took a long time at appeal to elaborate on how all the evidence stacked against his client was circumstantial. There was a forty-five minute wait for Wallace, before he would know if he were to hang or not. Lord Hewart had found three clear elements which had to be weighed and discussed: first, Mr Oliver had not said that there was no case to answer in the original trial; secondly, was the summing up done with accuracy? Third, as Hewart said: 'The whole of the evidence was closely and critically examined . . . The court was not concerned with suspicion, however grave, or with theories, however ingenious.' In using Section 4 of the 1907 Criminal Appeal Act, Hewart quashed the conviction.

The last word has to go to Wallace himself. He said: 'I hardly knew what it all meant. It seemed ages before he reached the sentence which conveyed to me the knowledge to step out of the dock, free.'

But the stigma is such affairs does not go away. By the end of 1932, he had moved away from Anfield and he was a sick man, with kidney disease. He died in Clatterbridge Hospital on 26 February 1933 and was buried with his wife in Anfield cemetery.

CHAPTER 32

Wartime Crime Tales

1939–54

The scam maestro took his own life . . .

The war with Hitler was so massive, reaching into the darkest corners of life on the Home Front as well as on the seas, in the air, and on land, that it inevitably invited unscrupulous types to exploit the situation. This meant much more than simply looting or appropriating government property to set up retail sidelines. At times it meant large-scale enterprises and a degree of violence in gang-land. Liverpool had its share, being a crucially important seaport.

First, there were the ordinary rackets such as trade in marketing restricted goods. In a world of rationing, this was not difficult to achieve. Some trading was significant, like the 1945 scheme to steal a large quantity of watches, pens and lighters, up to the value of almost £100,000. It might have come off, but for the fact that there were detectives planted among the crooks, as American staff from the army investigation division infiltrated, and in no time the British CID were stepping in.

When the Walker Art Gallery was transformed into the Liverpool Ministry of Fuel, underhand things began to happen, this time with clothing coupons. This involved crimes by female clerks and typists. This was happening early in 1944 and it took some time before the scam was discovered. In the end, eleven people were prosecuted and fined. The ration books for fuel coupons provided a fine profit, going from a value of just over £1, and then trebling in value at the Fuel Office.

Another easy source of income for the unscrupulous was the exploitation of the 'reserved occupations' – the categories of work which would exempt an individual from military service. Obviously, anyone who had the power and the means to switch or create identities could see to it that a man could avoid a battlefield by being classified as a minor, for instance. One man who was indeed in a position to profit from this was David Rowan, a businessman who was also on the city council. He indulged in

THIS WAS ONCE THEIR HOME—NOW IT IS A BATTLEFIELD.

A scene from the Blitz. *Liverpool Post*, 1943

forgery, false pretences and making chains of production of imitation documents for use in this way. Mr Rowan was given a seven year custodial sentence.

But the large-scale case in the war was the story of Frederick Porter. He was director of a company of ship-scalers and has been

Ruins after a bomb. *Liverpool Post*, 1943

What used to be South Castle Street. *Liverpool Post*, 1943

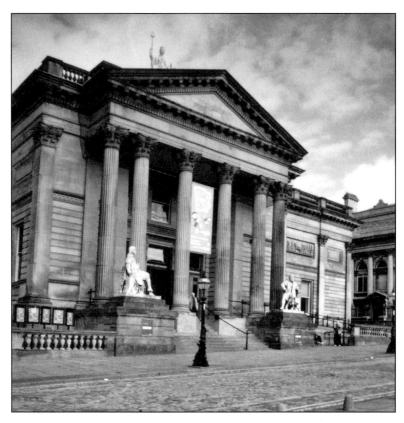

The Walker Art Gallery. The author

called a 'mastermind in crime.' His activities in fraud was of
mammoth proportions, reaching into Cumbria, and involving a
whole ring of powerful people in Merseyside. Porter had not only
made large quantities of cash, he was a master of storing and
stashing the money in various places. It all began with thefts from
Grayson Rollo and Clover Docks Ltd. The Porter ring had
exploited this timber and its retail, working sales into Admiralty
books. In only a few years Porter had made the huge sum of £20
million (in present-day value). As Donald Thomas has written,
'He could have financed the building of a warship out of his own
pocket.'

Porter's main method of 'sorting' the cash profits was to store
sums of money in strong-boxes in a string of banks. It seems that
large sums were also stored elsewhere and were never found. But

all this ended with Porter's suicide, just after an accountant from the Admiralty had paid him a visit and had seen some discrepancies. Porter shot himself that night, 30 January 1942. The scam maestro took his own life and the shady business had run its course.

The unfortunate firm of Grayson Rollo had more problems a year later, when there was more fraud. Amounts of money recorded as wages by staff were in fact never paid, but appropriated. There were various frauds committed in the ranks of workers, some of whom were recorded as working far longer hours than they actually did. A scam called 'Minesweeper' was blown by an honest man who blew the whistle on the plan. The operation involved small payments by drillers to their bosses, who would then record full days of working hours.

The black market in the war had many faces: even the somewhat farcical but clever business of making women's underwear from shrouds – clothing no longer needed by the dead of course. But main targets of crooks would always be food (particularly meat from the docks) and clothes. In the year 1941 alone, over 2,000 beef and lamb carcasses were purloined. Overall, crime rates in the war soared. The easiest booty was always going to be from looting after bombing, of course. But no one would have wanted to steal from one target – Walton Gaol – which was hit in September 1940.

Finally, there were much less subtle ways of taking some prizes from the situation, such as the notorious case of a troopship's galley which was smashed by some ship's cooks with axes one day in 1943; they stole a massive stock of bottled beer and whisky, and they also cooked a special meal for the soldiers. Many were found drunk and disorderly when an officer investigated the noise.

CHAPTER 33

Suicide in the Adelphi

1942

A morphine overdose was to end the life of this notorious aristocrat

I t is not widely known that the end of the story of one of the most intriguing and celebrated murder cases of the twentieth century happened in Liverpool at the grand and stylish *Adelphi Hotel* in 1942. It was there that Sir Jock Delves Broughton took his own life. The story was that of the

Two old images of the *Adelphi Hotel* interior.
Author's collection

murder of Lord Errol in Kenya in 1941, whose body was found in a car in January of that year, with a bullet lodged in his brain.

The irony of the place of his death is not hard to miss. The *Adelphi* is huge and palatial. A visit there now evokes the glamour and excitement of the great age of the ocean liners. In the 1940s it would have had some of that glamour. In the midst of the ball-room dances and the ebb and flow of immigrants and fugitives from war, the inscrutable old drinker and *bon viveur* exited the world. There is something fitting there in the effete and somehow pathetic figure dying in that place.

In the film *White Mischief*, the murder and the tale of the affair that caused it is told with high drama and passion. There were certainly elements of that in the real tragedy of this threesome of older man, attractive young wife and dashing lover. But there was also a large element of what we now see as sordid and sad. The affair is all the more fascinating because Broughton was the only real suspect and yet the murder is unsolved to this day. Broughton insisted on his innocence, writing to an aunt in 1941 he wrote, 'I was just a victim of unfortunate circumstances . . . some clever person took advantage of an unrivalled opportunity of getting rid of Erroll and . . . throwing all suspicion on me.'

'Jock' as he was known, had married Diana Caldwell in Durban in November 1940 at a registry office. From there they went to Kenya. He had promised to let her have £5,000 a year. Then she went on to enjoy herself with Lord Erroll, and Jock's torment began. There was something inevitable about the course of Erroll's life, from the affair through to his being shot on the Ngong to Nairobi road. What made Broughton so intriguing a character was the fact that he had been hired by MI6, and that he had a Somali driver who worked for him, leading to the theory that this driver could easily have been in the back of the car that night, and could have done the required execution.

Broughton's descent after the acquittal from the murder charge led him to Liverpool. He had always been a heavy drinker, but now he was intensely so, and he boarded ship for Liverpool in October 1942 in a rotten state. He was still full of venom, and cabled his friend Colville from the ship saying of his former wife, Diana: 'You've got the bitch, now buy her the kennel.' He was angry and vengeful, writing that he would let it be known that Diana had perpetrated an insurance false claim some years before. The desperate and raging lord must have felt that this was his final journey as he had only been in Liverpool for just over a month when he took his own life. A morphine overdose was to end the life of this notorious aristocrat.

The modern entrance to the *Adelphi Hotel.* The Author

Even in death, however, there was mystery around the man. The Liverpool coroner had been given possession of a letter written by Broughton to be given to him after the man's death, and the coroner never made the contents of this public. But with regard to the anticlimax of the manner of Broughton's death in Liverpool, it must be said that according to one line of thought, the whole thing was in fact a murder and had been fabricated as a suicide. The theory goes that Broughton knew too much from his past in espionage and in terms of the politics of the time and place of his life in Africa. The outcome, if we believe this speculation, is that he had to be removed from the scene, and that the OSS (Office of Strategic Services) had made sure that a particular drug was taken that fateful night. As Errol Trzebinski has said, the Liverpool coroner would have been expected to know where the fatal drugs came from. Perhaps he had no idea. What we are left with is a spy story, one involving a man who was maybe involved in a 'hit' job on Errol, but who was just a pawn. Here was a man who was suspected of being a fraud, and surely weighed down by guilt.

His character has been summed up by historian David Cannadine in this way: '. . . another dim and vain Etonian, with fifteen thousand acres in Cheshire and Staffordshire . . . . He evaded military service in 1914 on the grounds of sunstroke, and brought the Spring Valley estate in Kenya in 1923. His purpose in life was to have a good time.'

There was no good time that night in the *Adelphi* when he reached the end of the line. If it was suicide, it was a crime of course, at that time. Until 1961 that kind of death was an offence in the eyes of the law. The grand, palatial *Adelphi*, was the pride of the city in several incarnations since James Radley built the first one in 1826, including the version that was fairly new when Jock arrived – the delight of the great hotelier, Arthur Towle; who would have been shuddering with shame at the stigma of a suicide in those marble walls.

CHAPTER 34

The Cameo Cinema Case

1950

Whoever the gunman was, he left behind a mystery and a mess . . .

In June 2003, a verdict made in 1950 was overturned. That might not be such an amazing fact, except for the detail that the crime in question was a murder, and that the man who was hanged for that crime was now the victim of what is known in law as an 'unsafe' verdict. The man was George Kelly, and his remarkable story began in 1949, when cinema-goers were watching a thriller in the Cameo Cinema, Wavertree.

As the audience were engrossed in the film they were unaware of the drama going on in the back room. The cinema manager, Leonard Thomas, was in his office counting the night's takings. Mrs Jackman from the cashier's office took the money to Thomas and his assistant, Mr Cattrell. But as Mrs Jackman walked downstairs again, she heard six gunshots. When she ran back to the office, she found Thomas dead and Cattrell mortally wounded.

Kelly was stuck in the place with the gun. Connolly was very quick to get out of the building. Kelly then had to think of something quickly, and that was to buy a man a drink in a pub called the *Leigh Arms*. The problem was that the man was a stranger and he also saw that Kelly was out of breath and slightly excited.

This happened in March. Then in September, when there were no real suspects being investigated, Liverpool police had a letter in which the writer said he knew the names of the killers, and that if the police would place an advert in *The Liverpool Echo*, the results would be of great interest. The police were keen to make progress as they had questioned over 65,000 people. Intrigued, and willing to try anything at that time, the police did so. When the advert was placed, a man called James Northam rang the station and after that he met officers and told a story of how he overheard two men planning the robbery. They were George Kelly and Charles Connolly. Both were charged, and what followed was, at the time, to be the longest criminal trial on record.

Kelly was twenty-seven, a labourer, as was Connolly; but the 'grass', Northam, had also been involved. Other memoirs of Kelly refer to his earlier work as a 'barker' for an escapologist and even a deserter from the navy. The situation led to the first trial being indecisive. After thirteen days, the jury could not agree. Then, on 3 February, as *The Times* announced, the two men were to be tried separately. The newspaper account explained why, quoting Mr Justice Cassells: 'So far as I read the depositions, they seem to disclose that the two cases for the prosecution differ in fact and law and in some important respects. A separate trial eliminates all evidence which is not directly against the person being tried.' That time a verdict was reached: guilty. There was a murder charge against Kelly and his sentence was death. Connolly received only a ten-year sentence for robbery. Kelly was to hang.

An appeal followed, and Rose Heilbron, who had been born in Liverpool in 1914 and who became the first one of the first two women to take the silk in 1949, led the defence and stated the case. She was the first woman to lead a murder case. The issue, argued before Mr Justice Hilbery, was on the question of one of the jurors at the original trial having a previous conviction. If that person had been said to be unfit to serve on the jury, then that trial would have been void. Heilbron had clearly done her homework for in her speech at the appeal she went through various Victorian cases and statutes, with the argument hinging on the definition of the word 'attainted' Did it equate with the word 'convicted?' William Gorman, for the Crown, convincingly argued that the only cases in which a new trial would be granted were those where 'the identity of the juror were an issue.'

Kelly lost the appeal. The case was not referred to the Lords, and the last hope, a request for a

Rose Heilbron, QC. Andy Tennick

pardon from the Home Secretary, proved futile. The man in that position, Chuter Ede, had given a pardon not long before this, in a Newcastle case. But this time he did not, and Kelly had an appointment with Albert Pierrepoint.

In June 2003, three appeal judges announced that the 1950 trial was unsafe. The Kelly case had been handled by the Criminal Cases Review Commission. What had emerged is that a statement made by a witness at the time named a certain Donald Johnson as the killer. *The Guardian*, reporting this news in 2003, noted that Kelly had been known as 'a petty criminal named *the little Caesar of Lime Street.* Whoever the gunman was, he left behind a mystery and a mess.

The story that came out of this was that a prisoner, a man called Robert Graham, had been the killer; he had been released after implicating Kelly and Connolly. The amazing detail here is that it was not until 1991 that this was revealed, and that was when a researcher was given access to the police file on the case. It appears that Graham must have spoken to a detective called Balmer. Kelly had told Balmer in interview that he had never had a gun and that he did not know how to use one. Clearly, he wasn't listened to or believed. Balmer was a man in the centre of controversy in other large-scale Liverpool crimes as well. Frankie Fraser recalls him as 'the most famous copper in Liverpool a bit before and after the war.' He adds that Balmer 'Had three big cases and there's still trouble going on about one if not two of them'. We now know what an ironical understatement that is.

CHAPTER 35

After the Stash

1951

They set about their victim with a piece of wood . . .

yd Dernley, the former hangman, wrote in his book, *The Hangman's Tale* (1989) a neat paragraph that with hindsight is a wonderful understatement about this case:

> *The double execution was at Walton prison in Liverpool and went ahead amid extraordinary fuss and uproar from people who protested right to the end, and indeed, beyond, that we were hanging two innocent boys.*

The furore he refers to had involved a high profile enquiry into the possibilities of a miscarriage of justice. The two 'boys' in question were Edward Devlin and Francis Burns who had been accused of the brutal murder of Mrs Beatrice Rimmer in her own home at Cranborne Road, Wavertree. There had been word in the neighbourhood that Mrs Rimmer had been left a lot of cash by her husband and, as was a common habit in those days, she had not banked it, but kept it somewhere at home.

On 19 August 1951 she came home late and as she opened the door and stepped inside she saw that two men had tailed her and now stood before her, ready to do some harm. They set about their victim with a piece of wood and she was brutally beaten to death. Mrs Rimmer took a long time to die, but amazingly no-one in the neighbouring houses heard any disturbance. The next night her son came to see her, and he had the terrible experience of peeping through the letterbox to see the body of his mother outstretched in the hall. She was lying in her own blood, still clutching some flowers she had bought the day before. The poor victim had a dozen head wounds. The overall number of wounds on her body was fifteen, from two weapons which had been used. The killers had not been able to find the supposed money and it had driven them to a wild fury. They had broken in through a window.

There was a network of communications on the streets in a crime of this nature, and information soon led officers to the two young men, Manchester criminals: Devlin, aged twenty-two and Burns, twenty-one. They claimed that they could not have done the killing because they were doing a 'job' in Manchester that night. But there was a host of people with witness statements about the men, and they were charged.

The celebrated Liverpool detective, Herbert Balmer, went to talk to Burns's girlfriend, Marie Milne (known as Chinese Marie) and she told a tale of her being involved as a look-out but then that plan was abandoned later. It was also discovered that one early plan had been to use a local woman called Bury, who figured later in the enquiry, to go to Rimmer's front door and keep her talking while the two men went in through the back and looked for the cash. Obviously, for the fortnight between them being heard to talk about the robbery on the train and the day of the murder, a number of ideas had been discussed.

At their trial, they relied on naming a range of other characters who were allegedly trying to spread the blame. The two defendants were arrogant and abusive, both to the judge and jury. The public gallery was packed with curious citizens and there were long queues outside on the last day of the ten days of the trial, eager for the verdict. For the defence the men had Rose Heilbron and Noel Goldie – a formidable team. But the sheer conceit and bad behaviour of the accused was going to be an obstacle to effective legal work in the arena. But their expertise was to be tested later. At first the verdict was guilty and Justice Finnemore put on the black cap.

The case went to appeal and failed, but then, on 27 February 1952, the Home Secretary, Sir David Maxwell Fyfe, appointed Albert Gerrard QC to lead an enquiry to see if there had been a miscarriage of justice. This sprang from Rose Heilbron's handing a copy of a statement to the appeal court judge, and he said: 'It may be a matter for the Home Secretary in certain events.' The reason for this was that there were dozens of people involved who had all given garbled or partial statements regarding both the alibi of the Manchester robbery and about the possibility that the men had been framed. *The Times* reported the announcement in dramatic terms:

The Home Secretary has appointed Mr Albert Dennis Gerrard to inquire into the statement made on March 27 1952 by Elizabeth Rooke to the effect that June Bury and other persons had told her that the prisoners . . . had not committed the murder.. and that it had in fact been committed by another un-named person who is alleged to be the father of Bury's child..'

The aim of the enquiry was primarily to look into this statement made by one Elizabeth Rooke, the confession made by Joseph Howarth that he had done the murder, and a batch of other statements made to officers and to prison staff. The un-named person turned out to be a fabrication coming from Bury's strange tales of a man called 'Aussy' who was never traced. Gerrard stated that she was lying. As *The Times* reported about this woman's testimony: 'She knew or believed that the father of that child was one Edward Duffy, and that he was in prison at the time of the murder.'

At the Court of Appeal it emerged that a teenager, Rooke, had made allegations about the probity and reliability of a key witness, June Bury. The basic facts about the case in terms of prosecution were that the men had planned the robbery on a train journey from Manchester to Liverpool two weeks before the attack and murder. Another woman witness had stated that she had been with the men for three days around the time of the murder and had left them at the time of the break-in. Despite these accounts, the defence counsel were still seeking to establish that the men had the Manchester alibi: that they were breaking into Sun Blinds of Great Jackson Street on the night of the murder. There were six major statements to be checked out, most notably a supposed confession.

This had been made by Howarth. He had said that he had been in the home of Mrs Rimmer that night and had been hidden in a cupboard, waiting for her return. He said that he jumped out and hit her when she came home. It didn't take Gerrard long to dismiss this. Not only local police but Jack Spooner of the Yard had been to check this, and Spooner had made it clear that the only cupboard in the place was under the stairs, and on the murder night it had been full of household appliances – objects that had not been moved for some time, and so were in that space on the fateful night.

Howarth was in the opinion of Gerrard, giving the court the 'stuff of pure invention.' All through the inquiry, Gerrard made statements about how he formulated judgements about the reliability of the various statements.

Another player in the drama was one McLoughlin. Devlin had written a petition in which he claimed that when he had been picked out and his arrest confirmed, McLoughlin had been given a physical description of them both by a confederate called Milne.

Devlin said that he had never seen McLoughlin, ever. But McLoughlin had been in Walton for several days, and had made judgements at two identity parades. How did he get the prior information about the two men if he was inside?

Later, it emerged that Howarth had recanted his 'confession' as well; he was asked why he had told a pack of lies and could only reply: 'I heard a lot of people saying he was innocent and I sort of believed that he was innocent myself.' To D S Newton, Howarth said: 'I was canned up when I said it. I've never seen Burns in my life . . .'

The die was cast. Nothing in the long enquiry changed any opinion of the appeal judgement. The two men were to hang, and they had their appointment with Syd Dernley. It must have been a momentous statement when Mr Gerrard gave his decision:

> *I have examined this relationship very carefully. As a result I have to report that in my opinion there has been no miscarriage of justice.*

The very last gambit from the killers' lawyers was a memorandum begging for a reprieve from Her Majesty; but this came to nothing. Locally, there were still voices clamouring for a revision and that the men were innocent; then there were rumours in the popular press that the men had made death-cell confessions.

Dernley recalled that in their cells, the men were 'trying to play the hard men.' It's hard to believe, but he reported that even in the death cell, Burns was planning revenge on those who had spoken against him. On 25 April they were hanged. Apparently Devlin started to weaken near the end and the tough image dissolved. As for Burns, he was, said Dernley, putting up a front until very near the end.

Even this was not the end of this saga. On May 19, one G Rowland wrote to *The Times* after reading about the Lords discussing the point that the Court of Criminal Appeal should have the power to order a retrial. He wrote:

> *The surprising thing is that the Lord Chancellor said that any legislation to this end would certainly be controversial.*

Then he added:

> *. . . who, I would ask, is against this salutary reform?*

The two young killers had not only stirred up public indignation and created more open discussion of the death penalty, they had also pinpointed the odd process of having to ask the Home Secretary to order an inquiry into a possible miscarriage of justice.

Behind all the furore and the letters to the papers, though, what remains the powerful image of the Cranborne Road murder is the gallery of faces showing the people involved: Binns's photograph shows a hard face with set, firm lips; Devlin has a face reminiscent of the Teddy boys of the era. Finally, in the records there is the sad, ironically happy face of Mrs Rimmer, wearing a formal hat and smiling broadly.

CHAPTER 36

The Rugby Player Hero

1963

The snatch and coshing of two wage messengers was made by bandits using pick-axe handles . . .

eter Short, a quantity surveyor from Great Crosby, found himself in the centre of a violent heist in November 1963. He liked to play rugby and his fitness was very handy in doing what he did that day.

Six bandits arrived at premises in Great Howard Street and their sights were set on two Midland Bank messengers who had just walked out of the bank building as the villains arrived. The messengers, Stanley Smith and Norman Carter, were carrying cash in two suitcases. The snatch and coshing of the messengers was made by bandits using pick axe handles. The robbers took £3,500, but they made one mistake: they attacked their prey in front of Peter Short.

Short had been driving to his office when he 'saw people rolling around the pavement' and he wasted no time in following the men in their blue van, swinging his car into Lightbody Street to give chase. The villains threw building materials and buckets behind, to try to stop their pursuer, but he kept on.

A van somehow moved in between Short and the robbers, and still the missiles kept coming. He later reported that nails, wood and sand had been hurled at him. Finally, all this had some effect, as Short said: 'It was like driving through a dust storm but I still managed to keep the vans in sight. Then, after about half a mile around the back streets of Scotland Road a bucket thrown from one of the vans got caught up with my front axle.'

Many would have been deterred by this setback, but not Peter Short. He restarted and still had them in sight, finally seeing them run into a block of tenements. By this time, police were moving in and the place was surrounded. The robbers, it was later found, had used two vans and had left their booty – one attaché case contained £3,000; another bag was found near the first van, simply lying on the concrete.

RUGBY PLAYER CHASES PAY-GRAB GANG IN HIS CAR—AND THEY LEAVE £3,500

Express Staff Reporter

MASKED bandits in their getaway after a £3,500 wage snatched, scattered building materials and buckets in front of their pursuer, a 22-year-old Rugby player, through the back streets of Liverpool yesterday.

Warrant issued for boy, 11

A woman told Bury magistrates yesterday that her 11-year-old son, who was due to appear in court, had refused to get out of bed.

Said the chairman, Mr Robert Bradshaw: "If he won't come with you, we will get the police to fetch him." He adjourned the case for two weeks, and issued a warrant for the boy to attend then.

Nineteenth hole

VIRDEN (Manitoba), Friday.—Golfers here may meet hazards unknown on most courses—an oil well drilled between the first and third fairways.—Reuter.

Then they vanished—leaving their haul behind.

The snatch and coshing of two wage messengers outside their offices in Great Howard-street, was made by six bandits using pick-axe handles.

They were all masked with stockings over their heads.

The raid happened just after the Midland Bank opened in the street and the two messengers were leaving with the money contained in two suitcases.

Rolling

The messengers, Stanley Smith, 68, a wages clerk, of Ince-avenue, and Norman Carter, 40, of Rumington-road, Liverpool, were both taken to the Northern Hospital, but sent home later after treatment for head and body injuries.

The Rugby player, Peter Short, who is a quantity surveyor, of St Michael's-road, Great Crosby, said last night:

"I was driving into my office when I saw people rolling round the pavement. I swung my car

PETER SHORT
"Like a dust storm"

into Lightbody-street and chased men who I saw jump into a blue van.

"Then another van got in front of me and all sorts of things were thrown in my path.

"There were buckets, shovels, nails, wood, and sand.

"It was like driving through a dust storm, but I managed to keep the vans in sight. Then, after about half a mile around the back streets of Scotland-road a bucket thrown from one of the vans got caught up with my front axle.

Peter Short, the heroic rugby player. *Daily Sketch*

Smith, from Ince Avenue and Carter, from Rumington Road were taken to the Northern Hospital but were sent home. They were very fortunate, as coshes were nasty weapons, capable of doing terrible damage, such as fracturing the skull. In fact, attacks on bank messengers had been common over the previous fifteen years and, in 1957, after a case in Lincoln in which two robbers assaulted two young women bank messengers, the judge noted that 'This type of offence was increasing and becoming much too common and would have to be dealt with severely.' He gave a sentence of four years. No doubt the Liverpool attackers would have had a more severe penalty, as they had used offensive weapons which were likely to do serious harm to the victims.

But the story is dominated by the quiet man with his bushy hair and broad smile. He was just twenty-two and apparently afraid of nothing. *The Daily Express* made a major report of the case and he had a moment of fame, deservedly of course. The hero must have enjoyed the satisfaction of knowing that the robbers had got away with absolutely nothing for their trouble. What we don't know is whether Peter Short was given a reward by Midland Bank. He deserved something for that determined pursuit.

A Walton Gaol Tale

1946–47

Rowland's fate lay in the hands of the detective . . .

In 1947, Walter Rowland was hanged for the murder of Olive Balchin in Manchester. Rowland had had an alibi and also a man who could back that up. He had been to see his mother on the night of the murder, in New Mills. He had been picked up as he was on the list of Balchin's client: she was a prostitute. It seemed as though, in the first stage of the investigation, that Rowland had been in bed in Ardwick when the murder took place. But then a man in a Liverpool cell began to play a part in the story.

Mount Pleasant, where Ware was picked up. The author

HOME OFFICE

Enquiry into the confession made by David John Ware of the murder of Olive Balchin in respect of which murder Walter Graham Rowland was convicted at Manchester Assizes on the 16th December, 1946

Report by
MR. JOHN CATTERALL JOLLY, K.C.

Presented by the Secretary of State for the Home Department to Parliament by Command of His Majesty February, 1947

The frontispiece to the Home Office inquiry. Author's collection

A man called David Ware had stolen goods from a Salvation Army hostel, and now here he was, confessing to the Manchester murder. What was intriguing about this was that his written confession referred to a number of things that had not been reported in the newspapers, such as notes about the film Rowland said he had seen, and the fact that there was a ten-shilling note on the body. It was high profile indeed. The Home Secretary ordered an inquiry and a top-notch detective, Herbert Hannam of the Yard, went to Walton Gaol to talk to Ware. Rowland's fate lay in the hands of the detective and the Liverpool confession.

At first, Ware's statement was very convincing; he spoke of going to the bombed site (where the body was found) and

Hannam, the celebrity.
Daily Express, 1952

recounted his movements with Balchin in detail. The important statement was about that ten shilling note:

After I had felt this woman feeling in my pockets, I felt my trousers cash pocket and found that a ten shilling note, which I was certain I had put in that pocket, had gone.'

As Leslie Hale wrote in his book, *Hanged in Error* (see bibliography), 'This was not a statement to be lightly dismissed.' No one had reported that fact to the papers. How could Ware have known? After all, his first note to the prison governor at Walton had been bold, simple and powerful:

I wish to confess that I killed Olive Balshaw with a hammer on a bombed-site in the Deansgate, Manchester, on Saturday, 19 October, about 10 p.m. We had been to a picture house near the Belle Vue Stadium earlier in the evening.

Somehow, the detection team decided that the register at the boarding house where Rowland said he had been was said to have been tampered with, and that the man who ran the

Doctor X To Help The Yard

Hannam Seeks Two Nurses

"*Evening News*" Reporter

TWO doctors are to help Scotland Yard detectives in their inquiries into the Eastbourne deaths.

Their names are not being revealed. They are being referred to merely as Dr. X and Dr. Z.

Det.-Supt. Herbert Hannam, who is in charge of the inquiries, asked Dr. X to help last night. He made a preliminary statement, which he feels certain Dr. Z will corroborate.

Dr. X's information was about a woman who is believed to be alive and well following an illness at Eastbourne some years ago. Her present address is unknown.

It is understood that her London solicitors became concerned about her health while she was at Eastbourne and asked Dr. X to attend her.

When Dr. X saw the woman he agreed with an opinion expressed by Dr. Z, who had previously seen her and prescribed a course of treatment as a result of which the woman soon recovered.

Det.-Supt. Hannam is trying to trace two nurses. He was also trying to find the woman

Supt. Hannam asked Hove police to-day to examine the death certificate of Mrs. J. Butler, of Furze Croft, Hove, who died earlier this year. He asked for the details to be sent to him.

place had made a false statement. Ware had said that he had been to a pub in Oxford Street, Manchester on the fateful night. He described customers with telling detail; one man may even have been Rowland. Most important, he talked about buying a hammer (the murder weapon, according to Forensics) and then going to the pictures with Balchin. But Detective Hannam took Ware back to the cinema and jogged his memory. The conclusion was that the two apparently astounding facts that Ware seemed to know could have been easily available to anyone passing by. He had said:

> *I then went to a posh cinema which was about five minutes' walk away from Piccadilly . . . The cinema I went to . . . I paid 2s. 9d. for my seat which was well down the ground floor . . .*

The statement was crumbling and Rowland's fate was looking dismal. Rowland had no reprieve and there was no acquittal. He was hanged on 27 February 1947 by Albert Pierrepoint.

But in August 1951, David Ware told the police in Bristol that he had killed a woman. He added, 'I don't know what's the matter with me. I keep on having an urge to hit women on the head.' He was found guilty of attempted murder and, of course, he was quite insane. His favourite weapon was a hammer. Had the real killer of Olive Balchin been that 'madman' in Walton Gaol after all?

Sources and Bibliography

Books

Aughton, J., *Liverpool: A People's History*, Carnegie Press, Liverpool, 1990

Baker, J H., *An Introduction to English Legal History*, Butterworth, London, 2002

Benson, John, *The Working Class in Britain 1850–1939*, Longman, London,1989

Birkinhead, second Lord of, *F E: The Life of the First Lord Birkenhead*, Eyre and Spottiswoode, London, 1960

Bombers Over Merseyside, Liverpool Daily Post and Echo, 1943

Brabin, Angela, *The Black Widows of Liverpool*, Palatine, Lancaster, 2003

Campbell, Christy, *Fenian Fire: The British Government Plot to Assassinate Queen Victoria*, HarperCollins, 2003

Criminal Appeal Records, Sweet and Maxwell, annual (various volumes)

Davenport-Hines, Richard, *The Pursuit of Oblivion*, Phoenix, London, 2004

Eddleston, John J., *The Encyclopaedia of Executions*, Blake, London, 2002

Emsley, Clive, *Crime and Society in England, 1750–1900*, Longmans, London, 1996

Evans, Stewart P., *Executioner: The Chronicles of James Berry, Victorian Hangman*, Sutton, Stroud, 2004

Fielding, Steve, *The Hangman's Record, 1868–1899*, Chancery House, London, 1994

Forwood, William B., *Recollections of a Busy Life*, Henry Young, Liverpool,1910

Fraser, Frankie, *Mad Frank's Britain*, Virgin, London, 2003

Ffrench, Yvonne, *News from the Past 1805–1887*, The autobiography of the Nineteenth Century, Gollancz, London, 1946

Guide to Liverpool, 1902, Littlebury Brothers, Liverpool, 1902

Goodman, Jonathan (Ed.) *True Crime*, Paragon, London, 1999

Hale, Leslie, *Hanged in Error*, Penguin, London, 1961

Hawkins, Henry, *Reminiscences*, Nelson, London, 1904

Humphries, Steve and Gordon, Pamela, *Forbidden Britain 1900–1960* BBC, London, 1994

Isaacs, R., *Rufus Isaacs: First Marquess of Reading*, Hutchinson, London, 1942

Jones, D Caradog, *The Social Survey of Merseyside, Vol. One*, Hodder & Stoughton/University of Liverpool Press, 1934

Kilvert, Francis, *Kilvert's Diary, 1870–1879*, Cape, London, 1944

Lane, Brian, *The Encyclopaedia of Forensic Science*, Headline, London, 1992

Marriner, Brian, *Murder with Venom*, Pan, London, 2003

Melville, Herman, *Redburn* (1849) The Modern Library, New York, 2002

Midwinter, Eric, *Old Liverpool*, David and Charles, London, 1971

Nield, Basil, *Farewell to the Assizes*, Garnstone Press, London, 1972

O'Mara, Pat, *The Autobiography of a Liverpool Slummy*, Bluecoat Press, Liverpool, 1994

Pierrepoint, Albert, *Executioner: Pierrepoint*, Coronet, London, 1974

Porter, Roy, *Madness, A Brief History*, Oxford, 2002

Powell, Vincent, *The Legal Companion*, Robson Books, London, 2005

Slemen, Tom, *Wicked Liverpool*, Bluecoat Press, Liverpool, 2001

Smith, J F., *Liverpool, Past, Present, Future*, Northern Publishing Co., Liverpool, 1948

Stallion, Martin and Wall, David S., *The British Police 1829–2000*, Police History Society, Hook, 1999

Sugden, Philip, *The Complete History of Jack the Ripper*, Robinson, London, 2002

Thomas, Donald, *An Underworld at War: spivs, deserters, racketeers and civilians In the Second World War*. John Murray, London, 2003

Tibballs, Geoff, *The Murder Guide to Great Britain*, Boxtree, London, 1994

Tobias, J J., *Crime and Industrial Society in the Nineteenth Century*, Penguin, London, 1967

Trzebinski, Errol, *The Life and Death of Lord Erroll*, Fourth Estate, London, 2001

Veale, F J P., *The Wallace Case*, Clifford Elmer Books, Cheadle Hulme, 2005

(First published in 1950 by The Merrymeade Publishing Company, Brighton.)

Whittington-Egan, Richard, *Liverpool Colonnade*, Philip, Son and Nephew, Liverpool, 1955

Winder, Robert, *Bloody Foreigners, The Story of Immigration to Britain*, Abacus, 2004

Periodicals and Newspapers

The Gentleman's Magazine
History Today
Journal of the Police History Society
The Illustrated London News

Journal of Social History
Liverpool Chronicle
Liverpool Mercury
Morning Advertiser
Police Journal
Police News
Punch
The Times Digital Archive
True Crime Magazine

Audio-Visual Materials/Hypertext

The Lost World of Mitchell and Kenyon, BBC DVD
HYPERLINK "http://www.geocities.com" www.geocities.com
HYPERLINK "http://www.murderfiles.com" www.murderfiles.com
The Ultimate Price CD ROM from Paul Williams

Index